The Satanizing of Woman
Religion Versus Sexuality

The Satanizing of Woman
Religion Versus Sexuality

Demosthenes Savramis

Translated from the German by Martin Ebon

DOUBLEDAY & COMPANY, INC.,
GARDEN CITY, NEW YORK   1974

ISBN: 0-385-04485-2
Library of Congress Catalog Card Number 72–96232
Copyright © 1974 by Doubleday & Company, Inc.
All Rights Reserved
Printed in the United States of America
First Edition in the United States of America

Biblical quotations are from the Revised Standard Version
of the Bible, Copyrighted 1946 and 1952.

Contents

IV. SEXUALITY AND RELIGION

V. SEXUALITY BETWEEN RELIGION AND SOCIETY

Foreword

My extensive studies in the relationship between religion and sexuality indicate that sexual pleasure and its satisfaction contribute to interpersonal harmony and thus to harmony within all of society. Religion and sexuality must be seen as two strong life forces that should certainly not be regarded as antagonists.

This book is designed to document my theses by utilizing historic and contemporary data, drawn from the rich variety of information available in religious studies, sociology, anthropology and history. The reader will become aware that institutionalized Christianity has succeeded in creating, deepening and strengthening a rift between religion and sexuality that had not existed previously; this development has had most unfortunate results. I regard the exposure of this rift as a vital prerequisite to man's future rehumanization as well as for a dynamic renaissance of Christianity itself.

There exist, of course, a good number of books that deal with religion and sexuality. For the most part, however, these volumes are either exclusively concerned with Christianity or, more frequently, with only one denomination or with a single Church. Such works are often quite clearly normative in nature; that is, they are written from the viewpoint of a specific norm or set of standards. The few studies that deal with religion and sexuality in overall terms tend to concentrate on elements of difference and division between the erotic and the sexual. They are, therefore, likely to accept a Dualism between mind and body from the start, the very Dualism that caused a rift between religion and sexuality. This Dualism was also at the root of a morality antagonistic toward the sexual which actually caused much of the crucial religio-sexual rift with which we are concerned. This work differs from other studies in three major points: It is governed by the conviction that the scientist has no right to be a partisan of any one religion, even if a specific faith is, to him, equivalent to religion as such; we are not engaged in setting up norms for anyone; we define sexuality to include everything that may be among the satisfactions of human needs which grow out of man's nature as a sexual being. The end results of sexual intercourse, particularly those twin-guardians of morality—pregnancy and venereal disease—are side issues and should be treated as separate from sexuality.

This book is designed to show that religion, as an experience of the Divine, may function in unity with man's sexual activity. And we are using "Divine" as an overall concept of what is holy—*those* who are holy, or *what* is Divine—in an Encounter with the Divine, and as a Response to this Encounter that might manifest itself either through religious service or social action. Further, religion and sexuality are able to supplement each other. We learn from the history of religion, from ethnology and anthropology that wherever religion and sexuality coexist harmoniously, tranquility, joy, peace and true humanity are in evidence. Where, however, religion is at war with sexuality, we observe that a "civilization," notably the so-called Christian West, becomes the setting of events such as the Inquisition, the witch-hunts, the St. Bartholomew massacre or the concentration camps of Nazi Germany. Among the negative sex-related phenomena of the so-called Christian West stands the distortion of theology into a genitocentric rather than a Christocentric or anthropocentric (human-oriented) theology. This development has pushed Christ and Man to the outer periphery of theological concepts.

I shall develop and document these and related theses on the following pages. This book is written for a general, rather than an academic, audience with the specific intention of demonstrating to the young generation that a battle against religion in the name of sexuality is as negative as the battle of religion against sexuality. The war of sexuality against religion benefits only those who gain from the commercialization of sex. Among others who profit from this conflict are the antisexual moralists and their agents who attack the "sexual anarchy" in today's society, while they denounce and alienate the young generation because of its alleged straying from religion.

I   RELIGION AND
SEXUALITY

1. Origins of Sexual Pleasure

The people of Lesu, New Zealand, have a legend to explain the discovery of sexual intercourse. As reported by Hortense Powdermaker in *Life in Lesu*,[1] there was an original couple who had no knowledge of sexual relations. The husband regarded "his wife's genitalia as a big sore and was afraid of it." He asked a medicine man named Kutkut to heal it. The medicine man came, used one of his standard procedures (waving a leaf above the fire) and then asked the man to go down to the ocean beach. While he was gone, Kutkut had sexual relations with the woman. Just how and where the medicine man had discovered the right method of sexual intercourse, the legend does not tell, but we may assume that he obtained this knowledge from supernatural sources.

The man returned later and asked whether the sore had been treated, and his wife told him that it had been. But the husband could discover no improvement and he asked the medicine man twice more to treat it, and the medicine man used the same method. The man eventually got angry and accused Kutkut of deceiving him. The medicine man became furious, told him that his wife did not have a

sore at all and asked the man whether he did not know
what to do with her. He put the man into the proper position for intercourse, but he still did not know what
to do. This prompted Kutkut to pull a hot taro from the
fire and place it on the buttock of the husband, thus forcing him into action. The husband cried out, "Ah good,
very good, wonderful. I like it very much." And from
that time on, the people of Lesu knew about copulation
and valued it.[2]

There are many similar legends among so-called primitive people[3] that strike us today, depending on our moral
attitude, as amusing or dirty; but they certainly prove in
a very lively manner that pleasure in the sex drive is one
of man's original experiences. The legend of Lesu demonstrates two other things: First of all, it is a holy man who
acts as a magic priest[4] and who reminds us of today's
"men of God," who forces man to discover these pleasures
and to enjoy them. Further, there did not originally exist
any guilt feelings but rather a fear of woman on the part
of man—in this case fear of the "sore"—that might disturb
the man-woman relationship. At the moment man over-
comes his sexual fear, the other sex is totally accepted,
and there develops the basis for a healthy encounter between the sexes that, unfortunately, has been retained
only in archaic forms of society, among the so-called
primitive peoples. The sexual attitude of these people
remains the best proof that man experiences pleasure in
his natural drive as long as he can act free of fears and
pressures. The enjoyment of love encourages harmony
among men and therefore harmony within all society.
Religion and sexuality are two life forces we should not
view as antagonistic.

Anthropologists and ethnologists have amply proven

that most so-called primitive people regard sexual relations as "a natural and agreeable thing."[5]

II

Two studies should be especially mentioned at this point because they are recent surveys done without concern for the mixed feeling of the typical Western reader and, therefore, deal candidly and factually with the sexual practices of people in two different continents, Africa and Australia. The first of these is *Black Eros* by Boris de Rachewiltz;[6] the other, a work by Andreas Lommel, is *Progress Into a Void*.[7] We are indebted to De Rachewiltz for a most comprehensive study of sexual practices in Africa, documenting samples taken from the whole continent that African sexuality cannot be separated or isolated from the rest of life. But since primitive man does live in a world of religious myth that penetrates all aspects of life, it is only natural that his pleasure and enjoyment of sex are placed in harmony with his mythic-religious concepts of life as a whole.

The Munich ethnologist Lommel concerns himself with Australian natives who, isolated in small groups, retain a precivilization life style. The fact that these tribes have not changed their attitudes well into the twentieth century makes the Lommel report of particular interest and a rare contribution to this field. In contrast to De Rachewiltz, Lommel not only describes the sexual practices of his subjects but all of their culture. This enables him to observe how closely the sex life of the Australian aborigines relates to all segments of their existence as well as to their mythic-religious ideas. Lommel's report on Australia confirms the thesis, documented in De Rachewiltz's data, that sexuality may not be separated and isolated from the rest of a life pattern. In most primitive tribes, particularly those in Africa, life and the enjoyment of the sexual are nearly identical concepts.

The Australian aborigines regard the sexual act as "play" in which everyone engages "according to his power." This concept of sexual intercourse shows not only that primitives affirm the play functions of sexuality, but proves that the sexual act is a true partnership based on a free choice of partners. We may assume that these primitives practice a great deal of sexual freedom, but this should not be interpreted as promiscuity, which is actually nowhere to be found in so-called primitive societies. If we recall the choice of expressions now being popularly used in referring to the sex act, we may envy the primitive attitude. The expressions commonly used by Western people to describe sex clearly emphasize the brutalization of sexuality and the monopolization of it for male satisfaction; the splendid word "play" surely expresses the pleasure that can be the gift of uninhibited sexuality geared to the needs of *both* man and woman.

The so-called Christian attitudes cannot destroy the spontaneity and ease of sexual life among the primitives. Lommel describes how a missionary introduced him to his most successful pupil, "a gracious, slender girl who spoke excellent English and helped the teacher at the missionary station educate the children." Lommel writes: "I saw her in the afternoon in a brown sports suit. She was leading her team, and I had to admire the complete success of the English educational system. But this somewhat stiff English lady transformed herself at night, when the missionary was not present, into a passionate black woman, mistress of several young men—not only those who, under the rules of the tribe, were eligible for marriage, but

several others as well. The young men spoke of her glow-
ingly."

Nothing can better illustrate the fact than this little
story that our education has forced us into a hypocrisy
that has become a most important element of the civilized world. It forces two people of strong sexual drives,
who wish to live in a natural manner, to exist in an atmosphere of dishonesty; they are likely to turn into
neurotics or turn toward any number of perversions. The
anecdote just cited should help us to overcome the notion
that women are sexually passive, that they have no sexual needs. The sexual customs of all nations prove the
opposite: Women can be most passionate and active. In
Africa, for instance, a woman from the district of Rega
who meets a man in an outlying district, more or less by
accident, may offer herself to him without further ado,
and if he does not accept the offer, she and her girl friends
are likely to make fun of him.

Among the hot-blooded women of Africa are, according
to De Rachewiltz, the Babua, the Korongo and the Nes-
sakin from the Upper Nile. These people speak of their
free sexual relations openly and with enthusiasm. In Da-
homey, women who belong to a snake cult wear short
skirts which, whenever they meet a man they desire, can
simply be dropped. Hottentot women are particularly demanding in matters of love, and a Djisu woman who feels
unsatisfied may start to yell, so the whole neighborhood
knows all about it.[8]

Among the so-called primitive people, wherever the
man does not fear the opposite sex, men and women develop equal sexual desires, which they regulate and satisfy, free of pressures, on the basis of the principle of
pleasure or displeasure. The idea that a woman is a passive creature, lacking in sexual needs, is purely the prod-

uct of a male world which established rules of morality designed to monopolize the enjoyment of sex for men. In this artificial society, the "respectable woman" had many duties, was required to remain "pure," and had to hold herself in readiness to satisfy her man's needs. The highest recognition was woman's "honorable" role as a "self-sacrificing mother."

2. Toward Sexual Harmony

Whenever man is overwhelmed by fear of the opposite sex, he tends to create masculine societies characterized by homosexuality or other life styles antagonistic to sex. Wherever men live without women, or believe they can live without women, phenomena arise that may interfere with a harmonious togetherness of people. They glorify aggression in general and of war in particular, and the men tend to establish sadomasochistic relationships amongst themselves. Evidence left by past civilizations tells us that masculine societies which reject women on magic grounds become so involved with homosexual veneration of the penis and strong sadomasochistic impulses that these men find it impossible to accept sexual relationships, and in particular the sex act, as a matter of course.[1] We also learn from history that it does not much matter whether such masculine societies develop among the primitive (cannibals, head-hunters, etc.) or the "civilized" (ancient Greece and Rome, or witch-hunters, etc.).

A good example from primitive societies are the Papuas. On the one hand, sexuality plays a prominent role in Papuan life. On the other hand, their negative view of women is so strongly developed that they live in purely masculine groups whose practices are exceedingly cruel. According to Tony Saulnier[2] who made an expedition to the Papua, head-hunting is still practiced among certain Papuan tribes and is considered the main activity of these masculine groups. They express their strong sexual needs by egocentric means, particularly through the high value they place on their own genitals. During initiation ceremonies, for example, the head of an enemy who has been decapitated is placed between the boy's legs so that it touches his organs.[3]

Glorification of their own genitalia, resulting from a negative attitude toward women, can be observed even more clearly among the inhabitants of the island of Malekula in the New Hebrides.[4] Among them, the penis is considered the seat of masculine strength, and the men pay particular attention to this part of their bodies. Two categories of circumcision are practiced on this island. By one method, the foreskin is only split. In the other case, it is cut all around and then removed. Afterwards, the phallus is wrapped in several layers of palm leaves to make it appear enormous. The tip of the sheath is then placed under a belt made of bark, so that the testicles remain free. The wrappings may be as long as three feet.

Among the Papuas it is easy to detect the connection between negation of women and aggressive sadism. Among the inhabitants of Malekula it is equally clear that homosexuality and fear of the opposite sex are closely interrelated. For instance, one Malekula tribe indulges in certain "tricks" during the initiation ceremony. One of these has the older men wrap their penises with leaves until they take on enormous proportions. They then lie down in a row so that their enlarged penises form a continuous line above their bodies. The boys have to touch these false

penises and manipulate them. At the end of the initiation
period, one of the initiates climbs to the center of the
house occupied by men and asks the dead to appear and
have sexual intercourse with the newly initiated boys. It
is characteristic that the separation of men from women
on Malekula is so strongly practiced that the meat of a
sow cannot be eaten by men because it is taken from a
female pig. Furthermore, the common belief that women
have no souls and the fact that Malekula men are fanatical
fighters and erstwhile cannibals may serve as added evidence supporting the thesis that fear of the opposite sex
prompts the separation of men from women within male
societies characterized by aggression, sadomasochism and
homosexuality.

Among people whose sexual practices have not been
touched by Christian morality and who have overcome
sexual fears, there exists a harmonious relationship between men and women, expressed by a sexuality that is
regarded as a source of pleasure rather than as a burden.
These people furnish ample proof that sexuality, when
practiced according to natural norms rather than moral
grounds, is a factor that greatly enhances the harmony of
life. The reports by Margaret Mead from Samoa and the
findings of Bronislaw Malinowski on the Trobriand Islands
in Melanesia are of special interest here.[5]

Dr. Mead reports, for example, that masturbation,
homosexuality and unusual heterosexual practices are neither banned nor encouraged in Samoa. She notes that the
resulting ease of relationship prevents feelings of guilt
which elsewhere often cause adjustment difficulties. Varieties of heterosexual practices are accepted in Samoa, so
that individuals do not experience discrimination because
of their special needs. The fact that a wide variety of practices are regarded as "normal" creates an atmosphere free

of frigidity and psychologically induced impotence. Dr. Mead adds correctly that such an attitude, although not at all based on sexual contact without choice, tends to solve many other problems.

On the Trobriand Islands, the only known sexual taboo is a rule against sex relations with one's sister. Malinowski was unable to find a single Trobriand resident, male or female, who was "hysterical or even neurasthenic." Neither did he encounter any "nervous ticks, compulsory actions or obsessive ideas."

Only some thirty miles south of the Trobriand Islands are the Amphlett Islands. The Amphlett people are racially and linguistically related to the Trobriands, but their habits are totally different and so are their life styles. Premarital sexual relations are frowned upon in these islands; sexual freedom is not encouraged; family life is rigidly regulated. Malinowski found the Amphlett islanders "a community of neurasthenics." Compared to the open-hearted, easy-going people of the Trobriands, he found a society governed by distrust, "impatient at work, arrogant in their claims, though easily cowed and extremely nervous when tackled more energetically." When Malinowski arrived in native villages, women ran away and "kept in hiding for the whole of my stay, with the exception of a few old hags." He discovered quite a few neurotics whom he could not use as sources of information "because they would either lie in some sort of fear, or else become excited and offended over any more detailed questioning." Both Mead and Malinowski support the thesis of Wilhelm Reich[6] that a sex-denying morality causes neuroses, perversions and sexual dissociation; societies with positive attitudes toward sex do not experience such disturbances, because "in a society that provides sexual satisfaction, the social side of sexual relations is automatically taken care of."

A final example to support these theses can be found among the Eskimos, whose habits, from a viewpoint of Christian morality, may be regarded as shameless. Even though Eskimo life is governed by numerous taboos, particularly concerning birth, menstruation and death,[7] these taboos have not prevented the establishment of a sexually free society that encourages such practices as wife-swapping and sexual hospitality, ranging from Greenland to Alaska. But for an Eskimo, war is something "incomprehensible and repulsive" and his language has no word to describe it,[8] a fact that reminds us of the harmony among those who are sexually satisfied as compared to the aggression of those guided by morals that deny sex.

II

By closer observation of man's fear of woman, even among primitives—which plays a decisive and important role in sexual life—the magic-religious origin of such a fear is easily recognizable. It does not, however, have anything to do with sexuality and sexual intercourse. It was the results of sexual intercourse (pregnancy and birth) and menstrual blood that frightened primitive man and caused him to link women with the world of the gods and the demons, but it is for this reason that menstruation, pregnancy and birth form the main bases for the norms and social practices that exclude women from the world of males.[9] While sexuality, sexual intercourse and the enjoyment of the sex drive were not originally subject to magic-religious concepts, the results of sexual intercourse and the role of the female as a bearer of positive and negative religious power certainly caused masculine fears.[10]

This basic male anxiety continues to exist and continues to hamper male attempts to accept their sexuality as something that is pure and natural. While this anxiety, accompanied by more endorsement of the sexual, may lead to homosexuality, it is more likely to brand everything sexual as sin. Eventually, man objectivizes his fear by saying, "It is not that I am afraid of the woman, but it is she who is wicked, designing, criminal, a rapacious animal, a vampire, a witch, insatiable in her desire. It is she who personifies the uncanny and the dangerous."[11]

Alienation of the sexes from each other, caused by such fear of sex, can be observed in all civilizations and all forms of society. However, while among the primitive and within most non-Christian religions it is only fear that may keep man from satisfying his sexual drives, in the so-called Christian West, sex is further disturbed and poisoned by the addition of guilt feelings and the concept of sin. Among those outside Christianity, only fear separates man and woman; in the Christian West, they are separated by fear as well as by the degrading of woman as the embodiment of sin. While among non-Christians, sex fear hampers a proper synthesis of religion and sexuality, in the Christian West the synthesis is destroyed.

3. The Gods of Love

Eros and *the erotic* are concepts known to everyone today, while the terms *aphrodisy*[1] and *aphrodisiac*[2] are used mainly by psychologists and sexologists. All these words, however, have one thing in common: They originate in the area of religion and owe their existence to two gods, Aphrodite and Eros, both universal symbols of the harmony that could reign between religion and sexuality. Anyone who wishes to ban Aphrodite and Eros from the area of religion, arguing that these are simply "inventions," must remember that "whatever was once divine to man, remains divine"[3] and that one cannot qualify as a historian of religion without "re-experiencing in one's heart the belief in the Gods of the Ancient World."[4] Whoever, from the viewpoint of a specific religion, objects to the comparative study of all religions "is immediately open to the suspicion that he has something to hide; that his own belief is unable to remain steadfast while studying other religious concepts, or that he may wish to distort the evidence of history."[5]

Viewed in this manner, Aphrodite and Eros, together with the entire love life of the ancient Greek gods, are religious phenomena closely tied to the faith of the Greek people.[6] Of course, it is difficult for today's Christian to link the divine with the sexual. This does not, however, lie in the nature of the divine but in the fact that for hundreds of years Christianity has advocated "mortification of the flesh" as man's moral ideal and has satanized sexuality. Every child educated in the so-called Christian West comes to see religion and sexuality as opposing forces in such conflict with each other that the very idea of reconciling them becomes unthinkable, even blasphemous. Man is left with no alternatives but the choice of religion, at the cost of abandoning sex, or sex at the expense of religion. The non-Christian religions, however, provide excellent evidence that religion and sexuality are elements in life that cannot only be reconciled, but can supplement each other to benefit man and society.

Eros[7] is a cosmic primal force, one of the elements of world creation. According to Hesiod it was right after Chaos, the Endless Void, that Earth and Eros were created—Eros being "the most beautiful of all immortals, ruler of mind and feeling among all gods and men."[8] According to Parmenides, the Divine Creator "evolved first Eros among all other Gods,"[9] and Phaedrus refers to Eros as "a great God" admired by men and gods for many reasons, not the least of which was his origin, "since belonging to the oldest of gods is a great honor, to wit: Eros had no parents, and neither layman nor poet can name them. . . . Many, therefore, agree that Eros was one of the oldest. Since he is the oldest, we are indebted to him for the highest values."

The Christian West invented "platonic" Eros in order to diminish his power. But this spiritualization of Eros, which it thought it had detected in Plato's *Symposium*, has, as far as I can see, little or nothing to do with Plato. Let us first take a look at how the *Symposium* treats the myth of the male-females, the androgynes. Originally, there were three human genders, not just two as now, male and female. The third gender belonged to both of these. The man-woman, being male as well as female in appearance, represented the masculine as well as the feminine. However, this third sex angered the gods by its arrogance and ambition, and they decided to punish it. They cut it in half "as one cuts a pear to preserve it," and left the two separate sections in a perpetual state of yearning, each half searching for the other. This is the male-female myth. It tells us, first of all, of the yearning for the other sex; it then explains it metaphysically, giving Eros the task of leading man back to his original being, to join the two halves into one male-female, and thus to heal man's nature. It is true that Plato also seeks and finds solutions that will help man to exist without woman and woman to exist without man. The *Symposium* says, "Every one of us is a fragment of man cut apart, two instead of one, each looking forever for its counterpart; men who were part of this dual being, once called the man-woman, liked women. Most adulterers of this sex, be they male or female, remain forever in search. But women who were part of the Original Women do not care for men but turn toward women; the tribades[10] came from this sex, just as those who emerged from the purely masculine half search only for the masculine. As long as they are boys, they love the masculine in men. They enjoy lying with them and being in their arms. Among boys and young men, nature has made these most masculine. It is said that they are without shame, but this is a lie; they do not act shamelessly but with courage and masculine strength, attracted to those who are as they are themselves. Proof of this is that only they, as adults, become men of state; once they become grown men, they love boys; marriage and fatherhood are not of their nature; only society prompts them in this direction. They would be satisfied to live together, without marriage."[11]

The problems that result from the myth of the man-woman are not solved by Plato, who spiritualizes Eros and negates sexuality by preferring homosexuality to the heterosexual. He developed a metaphysic of homosexuality based on a purely physiological concept of Eros and reflecting the idea that the urge for a beloved being helps develop one's best spiritual powers. This speaks for a link between spirit and sexuality but not for a spiritualization of the sexual. Plato's defense of homosexuality, in terms of his own personal hostility toward women, testifies to the fact that the Greece of his time represented a masculine world whose relationships with the opposite sex had been disturbed. Not only Plato but many other notable Greek philosophers were known for their homosexual tendencies.[12] Plato's whole *Symposium* was, in fact, a drunken orgy of sensuality. Bruno Snell comments as follows: "The conclusion of the *Symposium* is a steep downhill road. The drunken Alcibiades not only praises Eros but also Socrates, exceeding what had been said before and leading back to something quite immediate and basic."

II

Sexuality, whether heterosexual or homosexual, was for the ancient Greeks a matter of religion. This explains why the "Golden Aphrodite" played such an important role in the life of both the gods and the men of Greece.[13] Even the story of her birth indicates this. It shows that the Greeks linked their gods, and thereby their religion, very closely to action, which the Christian West would regard as obscene. And, indeed, Aphrodite was not, as some hand-books have it, born of the foam of the sea; rather, she was conceived in the ocean by the enormous penis of the heavens (Uranus), which his son Cronus had previously cut off and thrown in the ocean. According to myth, "his part swam in the ocean for a long time, and around it was a white foam which emanated from this mortal part."[14] This penis was, in other words, filled with sperm which emerged from it and, with the ocean, created Aphrodite. Cronus had acted on the instructions of his mother (Gaea) who wanted to revenge herself for the fact that Uranus had robbed his sons of their power.

It was Aphrodite who presented both men and gods with the greatest gifts of life, the pleasures of love. Her work, and all the great works of the "Golden Aphrodite," can be identified with concepts such as lust, sensuality, yearning for the opposite sex, the erotic embrace, delight, beauty and life-as-such. The pictures of Aphrodite, and the cult of this goddess, show that not only mortal man, but the heros and immortal gods of Greece regarded her as magnificent. Behind this stands the Greek concept that in truth and nature the spiritual and religious are not alien to one another; thus, religion and sexuality cannot be antagonistic. Eros and Aphrodite remain eternal symbols of a world that did not think in dualistic terms and therefore was oriented toward a mentality I would like to call "nature-related harmony," as contrasted with a Dualism contrary to nature.

This Dualism, antagonistic to nature, is—as we shall see later in this volume—the result of a non-Greek philosophy, influenced by Far Eastern elements that sacrificed Aphrodite to antagonistic Dualism. We best see this whittling down of Aphrodite in the *Symposium* when Plato speaks of two Aphrodites, *Aphrodite Urania* (heavenly) and *Aphrodite Pandemos* (common). Then, because there exist two Aphrodites, there emerge two forms of Eros, including "the Eros who associates with the common Aphrodite, is truly common, exploits every opportunity, and is beloved by common folk."

We here encounter a new antisexual theme within a masculine society, an élite-consciousness manifested in the sexual attitude of men ranging from Plato to the advocates of clerical celibacy in the Roman Catholic Church. The idea that man is better than "womenfolk" or "common folk" encourages either homosexuality or total rejection of everything sexual. In my opinion, this élite-consciousness was used by masculine societies to justify their sexual fears, and it is this Dualism, antagonistic to nature, that we find in Plato's *Phaedo*. He writes that "the true meaning of the word enlightenment," the ultimate task of the philosopher, lies in the separation of soul from body.

Plato's conviction that men are much better than "womenfolk," and in particular that only men are capable of dealing with spiritual matters, eliminates the contradiction that might result from the fact that Plato, even though he favored Dualism, praised and endorsed homosexuality. While the Eros of the *common* Aphrodite is appropriate for the lower classes, capable of loving women, the Eros of the *heavenly* Aphrodite emerges from a goddess not concerned with the feminine but solely with the masculine. That is why this Eros governs the love of boys, and that is why those who are inspired by this Eros turn toward the masculine, which, according to Plato, is strong by nature and endowed with mental ability. Plato says: "Whoever is purely driven by this Eros, may be recognized by his love for boys."[15]

4. Cults of the Phallus

I

Before philosophical speculation absorbed the world of ancient Greece, it completely enjoyed the works of Aphrodite and Eros. Men and gods found pleasure in the beautiful, uncomplicated play of their bodies. One of the main characteristics of this society was the intensive love life it attributed to its gods.[1] Thus, Zeus, the Highest, God of Light and Father of Gods and Men, was a multisexual being who had many loves aside from his wife, Hera.[2] Zeus appears as "the heavenly seducer and benefactor of a seemingly endless number of mortal and immortal men and women, providing innumerable poets and artists with ever-new themes for sensual inventions. He also gave Hera ample cause for jealousy, especially when he carried off the beautiful Trojan Prince Ganymede and elevated love for boys to the very height of Mount Olympus."[3]

The son of Zeus and Hera, Hephaestus, God of Fire, personally experiences the results of Aphrodite's work. He discovers, through Helios, the all-seeing Sun God, that his wife, Aphrodite, is betraying him with the beautiful Ares. He thinks of revenge and welds strong and unbreakable chains that will force his wife to be forever faithful.[4] He

takes this chain, made into a net, secretly to his bed and
surprises the two together. Suddenly, they are caught in
the net, unable to move. Neither murder nor bloodshed
conclude this story, told by the gods on Olympus as a hu-
morous and amusing yarn. While the ancient Greeks did
not actually follow the example of Hephaestus, the Christians of Florence[5] imitated this pagan deity by inventing
the chastity belt, that mixture of sadism, dual morality,
emphasis on marriage through the sexual organs, and contempt for the female sex.

The God of Life and Pleasure, Apollo, is bi-sexually inclined and shows his preference for beautiful boys without
hesitation. His affairs with boys are mentioned frequently
in Greek mythology, and he was regarded as the Patron
God of Youth, who saw him as the image of the ideal lover.
His statue, therefore, was part of every Greek gymnasium.
But even here, in the adoration of Apollo, we discover that
the philosophers had a negative impact on the sexual life
of ancient Greece; it gave metaphysical legitimacy to
homoerotica, based on the Greeks' sexual fears. Even the
Greeks, who enjoyed a natural sex life, could not free
themselves from the notion that perfection could best be
found in closed groups of men; in a world without women.
Eventually, this antipathy toward women, born of the ancient Greek fear of the opposite sex, mixed with philo-
sophically based concepts antagonistic to all nature. These
concepts, in turn, infiltrated the Western world as a denial
of all that is of the flesh.

II

All the gods of the ancient Greeks, as well as their demi-
god heroes, demonstrate by their origin, their sex lives and
the cults surrounding them, that sexuality need neither in-

jure nor weaken man's religious feelings. For instance, Priapus[6] showed that the two powerful forces, sexuality and religion, can be brought together. As God of the Power of Conception and Virility, he needs to be particularly mentioned in this context. He makes us aware of undisguised sexual symbolism, the independent development of the sex organs into religious symbols. No longer was the god as such the center of religious ritual; it was his phallus that became the divine symbol of man's sexual life. Thus developed the phallic cults[7] that left traces all over the world. They achieved a transcendency of the sexual, making divinity real through the symbol of the phallus. Ritual acts, in which sexual intercourse or phallic representations form a central role, are not necessarily a form of fertility magic. They also had the religion-sociological function of demonstrating the "divinity of the sexual" to a younger generation.

If one observes the phallic cult related to Priapus, who is always shown with his penis erect, one observes that this cult is totally naturalistic in content—unless one regards it as purely obscene and negates it entirely. Priapus, together with Eros and Aphrodite, embodied a much deeper meaning; namely, that the principle of life and the principle of sex are divine entities of equal value. Yet, one finds the phallus as a religious symbol elsewhere, even on tombstones. The fact that the phallic sign could be found on memorials throughout Greece and Rome indicates that it symbolized eternal as well as earthly powers and meaning of the sensual. The phallus did not disturb a visitor to such a holy place as a cemetery, where it might decorate a grave. This proves that not the phallus as such but our present-day ideas of it, and of the sexual in general, are capable of hurting religious feelings.

As we shall see when discussing pornography later on,

obscenity is possible only in the Christian West, not in
a society such as that of ancient Greece which among
other things created statues honoring a goddess with the
name Aphrodite Kallipygos, "the goddess with the beautiful behind." Hans Licht notes correctly that it was only
possible in Greece to create the temple for a goddess "to
praise a part of the body for which we Germans do not
even have a respectable name."[8]

Sexuality and genitals played an important role not only
in religion, but also in the superstitions of ancient Greece.[9]
The Greek word *baskainein*, like the Latin word *fascinare*,
means not only fascinating or bewitching, but also the lifting of a witch's curse. Among the most feared curses of
ancient Greece was the Evil Eye, still feared in today's
Greece. Successful means of fighting off the Evil Eye were
pictures or reproductions of the genitals, preferably male
genitals. According to Licht, "The phallus may be found
nearly everywhere: on houses and gates; in public places,
quite often in enormous size; on utensils of daily life, such
as containers and lamps; on clothing and jewelry; on rings
and clasps, etc. It was also worn by itself, on a handle.
One thought to increase its influence by molding it into
the replica of an animal, such as a bird, complete with
talons and wings. It was occasionally fastened to a small
bell, as the sound of metal was regarded as effective
against magic and ghostly entities of all sorts. This explains
the habit of carrying phallic amulets, which the modern
observer, ignorant of its deeper reasons, might regard as
the ultimate shamelessness. . . . The Greeks ascribed
greater power to the male, and therefore his genitals were
seen as having greater effectiveness in fighting off the Evil
Eye. Instead of fashioning amulets in the form of female
genitals, they preferred symbols, such as a shell."[10] It was
nevertheless assumed that exposing the female parts

might break a curse, and so these were also worn in amulet form.[11]

Phallic cults and symbols are among the religious phenomena that can be described as universal. Genitals as parts of religious life have been found not only in Greece but also in India, where the male part is worshipped as an important divinity, and in Egypt, where Osiris appears as a phallic god. To this day, the phallus is linked with religion in such areas as the Congo and in certain African tribes, such as the Batju-Kulumwi in Rhodesia where the male organ is shown above temple gates and on altars. Among the Bantu, the phallic sticks of ancestors are stored in special huts. The use of phallic symbols in architecture, specifically as pillars, appears in the homes of the Djisu where they support the roofs of houses. There is a strong evidence that phallic cults are practiced in certain secret societies in West Africa such as the Ekangola, Mawungu, Chibados, Humoy, Muemba, Nyembe, Owis and Ramena.[12]

III

Let us now return once more to the Greeks and ask a well-justified question: How was it possible that, of all people, the Greeks—worshippers of Aphrodite and Priapus —developed an attitude so antagonistic to nature that it actually became the forerunner of a life style that denies all sexuality? Where did the ascetic tendencies originate that became part of declining Hellenism and decisively influenced Christianity? Let us note, first of all, that the world of Hellas remained a distinctly masculine society displaying the same antagonistic attitude toward sex that we find wherever women are viewed with disdain. Wherever man is unable to overcome his ingrained fear of

woman, he identifies her with all that is wicked and demonic and, consequently, turns against all sexuality. At
first, therefore, the sexes are not kept apart by feelings
of religious guilt or shame, but simply by male inability
to accept the quite-different female as a matter of course.
This results in an isolation of male society from the female,
which even though it resulted from a male inferiority complex, is advocated as based on masculine superiority. This
superiority manifests itself in the alleged ability of men
to live without women.

This results either in homosexuality or in a life style totally antagonistic to sex. Wherever fear of sex exists side
by side with a dualistic philosophical interpretation of life,
antagonism toward sex gains ground. Where harmony and
kinship with nature are pitted against the sex-antagonistic
Dualism, the forces directed against nature and sex are
likely to win out, particularly where they offer a release
from the disappointments of day-to-day life. This was true
in ancient Greece. Orphic religion[13] and the successive
philosophies of the Pythagoreans,[14] the Stoics[15] and the
Neoplatonists[16] were the milestones in a development that
began with the slogan, "the body is a prison," and ended
with a blending of the dualistic attitudes into the Western
world structure that forced men to agree with the philosopher Plotinus[17] who confessed that he was ashamed to
have a body.

5. Religion and Sex in Harmony

The facts surveyed thus far enable us to say that as long as man listens to nature and to his heart, and ignores philosophical speculations antagonistic to nature, he will never encounter conflict between his religion and his sexuality. On the contrary, the religion of those who have sought and found revelation of the divine in nature and in their own heart consists of myths, symbols, rites and instructions for daily living which we, who live in a so-called Christian civilization, are prompted to regard as "immoral," "obscene" or "unnatural."

Wherever man listens to nature and his own heart, finding in them the main criteria for action, he is spontaneously attracted by the other sex and seeks union with it. The histories of non-Christian religions offer proof that man's eternal sexual yearning need not distract him from religious experience and functioning. Religion and sexuality are two powerful life forces able to coexist and to supplement each other.

This is not only true in so-called primitive religions. We have already seen that the Greece of Homer saw nothing objectionable in the natural love life of its gods and he-

roes. In addition, a rich variety of examples from tribal and
world religions testifies to the same harmonious relationship between religion and sexuality. There exists an essay
on secret sexual practices in Chinese Taoism,[1] just as we
find a record of the Indian art of sex in the classic *Kama
Sutra*,[2] a prime example of sexual actions consistently
close to nature. Kalyanamalla, author of the *Anangaranya*,
the key work after the *Kama Sutra* in the erotic literature
of India, envisions the art and enjoyment of love as the
main guarantee of eternal happiness for the individual and
the world, because the art and enjoyment of love support
harmony among men and thereby harmony of human society. Let us also remember the erotic sculptures in the
Temple of Konarak which, as *Newsweek* once put it, could
arouse even the very old to "fiery yearnings of lust."[3]

India traditionally views sexual energy as a creative
force. It therefore endorses it as a basis of all life and,
to purify it from images that might be detrimental, seeks
to sanctify sexuality. Unfortunately, however, this is not
true of today's Indian youth, who experience conflicts
through sexual repression based on profane rather than
on religious considerations. Modern India provides a phenomenon that is strangely relevant to our basic theses:
Even in modern India, certain religious convictions still
regard the sexual as sacred; at the same time, there exists
a profane or secular "morality" that has all the earmarks
of antisexual attitudes in our Western civilization.[4]

II

If there were no other ways to prove our thesis that
religion and sexuality are compatible, it would be sufficient
to consider only the two great monotheistic religions, Islam and Judaism. Both provide excellent evidence that re-

ligion and sexuality are necessities of daily life that may be satisfied simultaneously. Above all, both Islam and Judaism strongly support the thesis that belief in a single God and the living, personal contact with Him need not suffer from intensive and deeply enjoyable sexual activity.

Islam endows sexuality with a metaphysical glow. We find in Sura 56 of the Koran[5] much evidence of this. Even the fact that Sura 44[6] says a man should have no more than four preferred wives quite evidently does not mean a man must limit his sexual activities. For one thing, the number four appears to have been Mohammed's favorite figure. Also, in his own life, the prophet set an example which clearly shows that the Mohammedan need not be bothered by his conscience if, in addition to his wives, he keeps an unlimited number of concubines.[7] Sexuality, as endorsed by the Koran, conquered all of the Arab world, which thanks Allah for its pleasures and praises him with such words of passion as, "Allah be praised, for He created woman for the greatest enjoyment of man and man for the greatest enjoyment of woman. He grants the woman's body her satisfaction only when she unites with the body of a man; similarly, man knows neither peace nor tranquility until he achieves ultimate union with woman."[8] Such works as *The Book of the Foundations of Desire, Tales of One Thousand and One Nights,*[9] *The Perfumed Garden of Sheik Nefzaoui,*[10] the *Book of Reisat's Games* or *The Book of Much-praised Slaves* include details concerning the sexual practices and sexual attitudes of the Arab world.

However, when we read in the Koran, "Women are your plowing fields; visit your fields, how and when you desire,"[11] we discover among the religiously legitimized enjoyment of sex an important negative factor that may decisively disturb a person's sexual functioning. We en-

counter disrespect, enslavement, and debasement of the
female into a "thing," which makes an "I-Thou" relationship among the sexes impossible. This attitude may be
encountered wherever—as in ancient Greece—patriarchal
prejudices conspire to proclaim the male as "master of
creation." The Arab world's disdain for women and its
brutalization of the sexual is clearly revealed in the Is-
lamic proverb, "A boy for pleasure, a woman for offspring."[12] This reaffirms our thesis that wherever the
male becomes subject to fears of the opposite sex, there
arises a male society whose main characteristic is either
homosexuality or a life style antagonistic to sex in general.

Arab fears of woman are expressed, among other
things, in the conviction that women are "impure," as
well as in the fact that contact with a woman is regarded,
as a rule, as dangerous if not disastrous.[13] The faithful
Moslem suffers from fear of the opposite sex, although
not from a general sexual anxiety. His religion has remained free of dualistic ideas, which might have turned
him against nature and body, so that he suffers no guilt
feelings when sexually active. Thus, even though Islam is
a religion of men who view woman with disdain, it does
not identify "demonic" aspects of the female nature with
sex in general.

III

Judaism regards man's sexual life at least as positively
as does Islam. The Old Testament offers a treasure of examples to show that the Jews welcomed sexuality as God's
gift, to be used fully. Solomon, who had "seven hundred
wives, princesses, and three hundred concubines,"[14] provides the classic example of intensive sexual activity within

a sexually oriented society. The Old Testament reflects also the enjoyment of the sexual drive that is excellently expressed in the proviso, "When a man hath taken a new wife, he shall not go out to war, neither shall he be charged with any business; but he shall be free at home one year, and shall cheer up his wife which he has taken."[15] This rule does not permit the newly married to be exempt from war service in order to insure national fertility, but to enable the man to live happily with his wife and to enjoy their relationship—a point to be carefully pondered by those who maintain that the positive attitude of Judaism toward sex was based solely on a concern for the perpetuation of a chosen people.

While it is true that the Jews viewed marriage as primarily a means of human perpetuation and regarded the family highly while they deplored the unmarried,[16] Jewish laws did not limit a man's sexual activity either before or during marriage. As long as he did not covet his neighbor's wife, he was free to enjoy sexual pleasures and freedom. The Old Testament's injunction against coveting the neighbor's wife was designed to protect the neighbor's property rights; in other words, it sanctioned the masculine law that regarded the woman as man's property. The man becomes an adulterer only when he covets the woman who is his neighbor's property. While an intrusion on another's marriage is punishable, breaking away from one's own marriage is accepted as a matter of course.[17]

As did most Oriental people, the ancient Jews regarded woman as chattel or part of the man's private property. Here, too, disdain for woman grew from a fear of women clearly felt by the males and demonstrated by numerous Old Testament passages that demonize the female. Thus, woman is variously described as "more bitter than death" and as a "trap," while her heart is a "snare" and her hands

are instruments of "bondage." We read that "whoso pleas-
eth God shall escape her; but the sinner shall be taken
by her."[18] Small wonder that only men are allowed direct
contact with the divine.[19] The high regard for virginity[20]
reflects man's right to regard woman as a property that
must, at all costs, be kept in the best possible condition.

We find ourselves, nevertheless, in agreement with Derrick Sherwin Bailey who, despite the evident limitations
and imperfections of Jewish sexuality, regards it as unex-
celled when compared with other ancient civilizations.[21]
Goethe valued Solomon's "Song of Songs" as "the most
magnificent selection of love songs created by God."[22]
He reminds us that the Old Testament speaks of possibilities open to every man capable of accepting religion and
sexuality as equal life forces that can be mutually sup-
portive. Neither contact with foreign cultures in exile nor
Hellenistic influence could destroy the harmony with nature offered by Judaism. At the time of Christ's birth only
a few small ascetic sects within Judaism were influenced
by dualistic ideas. On the whole, Judaism remained faithful to the sexual ethic provided by the Old Testament,
which knows only such laws in the sexual area as have
resulted either from fear of women (such as the magically
motivated cleanliness duties) or from the servitude of
women (such as punishment of adultery), neither of
which is based on religiously motivated feelings of guilt.

However, what neither Dualism nor a morality antagonistic to sexuality could create within Judaism was
achieved by law. The Talmud forced men into submission to the letter of the law, so that Jews lost their freedom
and permitted the law to control every detail of their life.
The law also killed enjoyment of the sex drive. The more
it is subjected to rules and taboos, the less can the individual enjoy his sex life. From a blend of magic-born

purity rituals, regulations insuring the servitude of women developed an all-powerful law that not only colored the entire criminal law in Judaism, but also left its stamp on the entire world we now describe as Christian. This judicial pattern obliterated any resemblance to the happy harmony between religion and sexuality originally expressed in the Old Testament.

II RELIGION AGAINST SEXUALITY

6. Christianity and Sex

Most errors and misconceptions concerning Christianity develop because people do not distinguish, either knowingly or unknowingly, between Christianity and its institutionalized Establishment, such as the Churches.[1] Therefore, I must discuss the subject of Christianity and sexuality quite separately from any associations between theology and sexuality, or between Church and sexuality. This makes it necessary to seek the purest form of Christianity. Such a search inevitably leads us back to Christ himself, for whom the whole movement was named. The only way to truly understand Christ's attitude toward the sexual is to consider it within the framework of his total teachings.[2]

When a sociologist studies the teachings of Christ, he concerns himself basically with those aspects of the New Testament that could have concrete sociological significance. When he approaches Christianity, his first task is to single out specific New Testament passages essential to Christian theology, as well as significant to society in general as it was and as it remains today. In my opinion, one such passage is the sentence, "The old has passed away, behold, the new has come."[3] This sentence is not only important because it views "the new" in terms of social change; it is also important because the statement is so radical that it makes two further questions mandatory. First, did Christ establish a new program for social renewal, a new morality or even a new legality? Second, what is really meant by "new," and how does this newness differ from the old that was past?

I believe that the following hypotheses may help to answer these questions. Christ did not establish a concrete program, a concrete morality or a concrete law. His struggle against prevailing social injustices was undertaken in the religious area, and certainly not in terms of social economics. Nor was Christ a social utopian; he did not expect that his teaching would change society immediately. And, finally, any attempts to formulate concrete socioeconomic, political or other systems would have contradicted the basic truth that wherever "the Spirit of the Lord" prevails, "there is freedom."[4] The history of theology and of the Church teaches us that whenever Christendom appears as a concrete socioeconomic, political or similar program, it deteriorates into an instrument of man's rule over other men.

While the teachings of Christ do not offer a concrete program, or a concrete morality for the renewal of society, they do establish prerequisites that may lead to the elimination of social injustices and the development of a new society. Among these prerequisites, the first is the *new man* whose faith will enable him to free himself from all compulsion and let him devote his entire strength to the renewal of the world in the Spirit of Christ.

Compared to the pre-Christian world, the society Christ envisioned emerges as a world in which every person, regardless of social or other background, represents the highest value imaginable. All the other material and ideal values serve only to help man in his efforts to achieve full self-realization. Thus, the concept of *love* achieves a very particular meaning; a meaning that did not exist in pre-Christian society. Christian love lifts all barriers that separate men and makes it possible to eliminate egoism; even the *collective egoism of the state.*

The Cross symbolizes the price Christ had to pay to the powers of the world in order to liberate his fellow man from all compulsion; the Resurrection symbolizes the victory he gained on behalf of man's subjective and objective nature. Thus, the gist of New Testament theology consists of the good news that man, thanks to Christ's death and resurrection, has indeed been enabled to change himself and therewith his world in a basic or a *revolutionary* manner.

According to New Testament theology, the Church must be a community of the faithful; a Church office or official can exist for no other reason but to be a servant. The Church leader as an *authoritative ruler* is but one of many products of later theologies and Church traditions that grew out of a blend of *post-Christian factors* and developed at the price of a constructive and joyful character of the true New Testament theology.

II

As for our thesis, a number of important points can be derived from the totality of Christ's teachings. Christ did not define a specific sexual ethic valid for all time. Such an ethic would have contradicted his major intent, which was to liberate man from all restrictions and would have run counter to his basic view which opposed all external legalities. Just as the Sabbath was made for man, not man for the Sabbath,[5] so were law, morality, marriage, etc., created for the sake of man, and not man for the sake of law, morality or marriage. Man who, according to Christ's teachings, is the supreme value, remains the only criterion as to whether a value system is Christian or not. Consequently, man is the only criterion by which we can measure the value of a given morality or even answer the question whether morality, as understood today, should exist at all.

The Incarnation of Jesus implies the potential elimination of all evil and the reconciliation not only of God to mankind but also of man to nature. Therefore, the Incarnation can neither eliminate nor even weaken the pre-Christian harmony between religion and sexuality. On the contrary, this harmony achieves new meaning as it becomes part of a new and redeemed world. Viewed in this manner, our time—a time that can be considered the product of man's liberation from all restrictions[6] and that even created the technique to liberate man from the consequences of love-making—may be regarded as the time for man's total liberation from the restrictions that have so long poisoned his sexual life and disturbed the harmony between man, religion and his sexuality. Among these restrictions are all laws made to control man's sexual life, by physical or other force, in order to shape it according to a specific morality. At a time when, thanks to scientific progress, indulging in one's sensuality can do neither biological nor social harm, such laws and such morality become superfluous.

The life and the teachings of Christ, we are convinced, had only one purpose: the elimination of man's unwholesome situation, by means of a faith that liberates from all others. An ethic can be labeled Christian only if it deals with the person as a whole, aiming to heal both spirit and body so as to make the person truly free. Thus, any morality that causes an unwholesome situation cannot be Christian. The sexual morality invented by theologians and the Church has, therefore, nothing to do with either Christ or his teachings. Quite apart from the fact that the gist of this morality is of pagan origin, it has caused endless harm by its attempts to enslave man while putting him at the mercy of laws incompatible to his nature.

III

Christ had very little to say concerning the concrete matters related to man's sexual life. The few observations he made concerning marriage and sexuality[7] do not reveal any antagonism toward sex. It is, however, only possible to interpret these remarks properly if we view them within the framework of Christ's total teaching and remember that Christ was a Jew; although he wished to humanize Jewish law, he accepted this law as part of his social environment. As we have seen, he did not act as a social reformer. Christ's social environment viewed woman as man's property. Jewish society at the time of Christ regarded marriage as a means of procreation, paying little attention to its role in satisfying sexual needs. Bailey has noted that the Greeks and Romans, like the Jews, regarded biological reproduction as the specific aim of marriage. He writes that the aim was the creation of legitimate offspring (meaning, children with the status of citizens) designed to serve the state and the cult of the gods. To this end, the law demanded formal monogamy, while society tolerated man's dual morality, including a sexual morality that accepted and excused prostitution.[8]

In this respect, Christ humanized the laws and habits of his society in two ways. First, he improved woman's position by making divorce impossible for women as well as men.[9] This was a clear-cut attempt to protect women against the arbitrary action of men who had previously been able simply to "dismiss" their wives.[10] Further, he freed men from compulsory conception when he emphasized that a husband leaves his parents to become "one flesh"[11] with his wife. This placed major emphasis on sexual union rather than biological continuity.

Christ acknowledged the governing attitudes of his time which viewed the wife as man's property. This is indicated by his observation, "Whosoever looks at a woman lustfully has already committed adultery with her in his heart."[12] This refers to lust for the property of another. Why, indeed, did Christ not also say "Any *woman* who views a man and desires him, has committed adultery in her heart"? The underlying meaning of this phrase can be found in the fact that Christ was essentially concerned with an inner world; with the motives behind man's thoughts and actions. In the world of the sexual, this means that legality and morality cannot be separated; whether or not we act correctly, what is decisive is our inner attitude towards our partner. That Christ cared little about pure legality can be seen in his judgment on the "woman taken in adultery."[13] Whereas the scholars and Pharisees backed a law that specifically demanded that such a woman be stoned,[14] Christ decided against the law and in favor of the adulteress; to him, the human person was simply more valuable than any morality.

Christ's life and teachings clearly show that he was neither an ascetic nor fearful of the opposite sex. His personal contact with women[15] reflects his convictions that both man and woman are of divine origin[16] and therefore equal. According to Luke, "Soon afterward he went on throughout cities and villages, preaching and bringing the good news of the kingdom of God. And the twelve were with him, and also some women who had been healed of evil spirits and infirmities: Mary, called Magdalene, from whom seven demons had gone out, and Joanna, the wife of Chuza, Herod's steward, and Susanna, and many others, who provided for them out of their means."[17] Other Scripture passages may be cited, such as that "Jesus loved Martha and her sister,"[18] or the fact that his disciples "marveled" at the manner in which he dealt with women,[19] to show that Christ was free of sexual anxiety and that his attitude in this, too, separated him from those around him. Christ thus differs from those who call themselves Christians, who use Christ's name to justify their fear of women, and who seek to propagate their attitude as if it were the normal condition of every Christian.

7. Theology and Sex

Church teachings on a "theology of sexuality" have one
thing in common: They all differ from Christ's original
teachings. Two additional elements stand out: They have
done only harm, and they mingle pre-Christian and non-
Christian views. Among their major characteristics are
these: Dualism, sexual anxiety, women seen as evil, sex
as Satanic and sinful, antagonism toward the sexual, con-
finement of sex to marital monogamy and sex justified exclusively for the purpose of procreation.

Dualism originated in pagan Greece. Sexual anxiety that
equates woman with evil is based on ancient magical concepts. The patriarchal viewpoint that led to sexual anxiety
led to a "theology of sexuality" based on a masculine society that could not cope with women and sex; both were
taboo, satanized or simply avoided.

This "theology of sexuality" shares contempt for woman
with the Old Testament and Islam. But while Judaism and
Islam limit sexual anxiety, the "theology of sexuality" reflects an anxiety about everything sexual that is based on
fear of the female sex. Christian theology adopted its tyranny of law from Judaism. Consequently, it established

a "morality" or "ethic" that made man into a slave of the law, forcing him to fit his religious and sexual life into a pattern antagonistic to nature. This "theology of sexuality" adopted its purely negative concepts of sexuality from non-Christian and pre-Christian societies. Marriage and women originally were positive elements in Christ's teachings. Only later were they so transformed that pre-Christian and non-Christian negativisms could be called "Christian." The names of two theologians stand out in this metamorphosis: Paul the Apostle, and Saint Augustine.

The roles of Paul and Augustine differ substantially. Paul's teachings had results he had neither planned nor foreseen. Also, his underlying personal antagonism to sex was not as obvious as Augustine's. If one sees Paul's view on marriage and sex within the overall context of his teachings, he certainly does not emerge as the father of Christian asceticism. Essentially, he advocated love of man as well as of Christ. To put it another way: Paul's theology is Christocentric and anthropocentric, but certainly not genitocentric. Augustine, on the other hand, did develop a genitocentric theology. He thus became, in intent and result, the true father of a "theology of sexuality" that concentrated on man's genitals rather than on man as a whole.

II

Paul[1] examined the concept of love with a thoroughness and depth similar to his concept of faith. One may refer to Paul, without exaggeration, as the Apostle of Love. Various translations use either "love" or "charity" in relating Paul's teachings, but the meaning is identical. The idea of such love appears in Paul's writings more than sixty times. This occurs when Paul deals with two subjects: love of Christ the Redeemer[2] and God[3]; and that of man's neighbor. He sees love as capable of transforming human nature, of adding new aspects of character to man's personality. Thus, love may express itself—in the form of love for God—through gratitude,[4] trust,[5] devotion[6] or prayer.[7] According to Paul, all of law finds fulfillment in loving one's neighbor, and all the commandments "are summed up" in the sentence, "You shall love your neighbor as yourself."[8]

Love, according to Paul, "binds everything together in perfect harmony."[9] Whenever the teachings of faith do not conform to love of one's neighbor, they lose their Christian meaning and impact. Evil forces quickly gain the upper hand[10] wherever hate replaces love in human society, so that "times of stress"[11] threaten such a society. Paul pictured a loveless society with striking realism. He viewed all other values in relation to love. Although civilizations, laws, manners and morality may change or disappear, "love never ends."[12] Peace may be gained where there exists its main basis, that of one human being's love for another. Love destroys such enemies of peace as envy, anger and aggression.[13] At the same time, love permits the unfolding of such qualities as tolerance,[14] patience and sacrifice.[15] These virtues open the path to peace and to a new existence where we "bear one another's burdens."[16] Unity, according to Paul, is also based on love; he sees loneliness and isolation as results of unloving selfishness. Love and selfishness are mutually exclusive; they contradict one another and are incapable of existing side by side. Love is never self-centered and, as Paul saw it, rules out all forms of egoism.[17]

Paul's ethic differs from pre-Christian ethics by precisely this view of love as basic and central. The later Stoics, notably Seneca, Epictetus and Marcus Aurelius, expressed views similar to those of Paul. But they did not

come close to his advocacy of love as a central element
in his teachings. We must therefore agree with Albert
Schweitzer that, where meaning and impact of love are
concerned, Paul's ethic is "comparable to none other than
that of Jesus."[18] Paul's teachings on love are unequaled.

Paul reminds us, in his First Letter to the Corinthians,[19]
that Christ's new world, created by his sacrifice, is founded
on love, which is the basis of relations between all men
and between all groupings that wish to regard themselves
as Christian. With some exaggeration but nevertheless
brilliantly, Paul attempted to ascribe to love the ultimate
and highest value. Even faith, which played an outstand-
ing role in Paul's ethic as man's only possible attitude toward God, loses all meaning without love. Faith and love
are not alternatives. Unless they exist together, there can
only be disintegration.[20] The First Letter to the Corinthians outlines the different qualities of love, as well as
its role in human society.[21] This supports our concept that
Paul's views on love are so all-embracing that they are
unique among teachings on human action.

Paul's views of marriage and sexuality lose significance
once they are viewed within the framework of his total
teachings. Their timeless nature is revealed when we recall that wherever the spirit of Christ might be found
"there is freedom."[22] Paul's teachings have also tran-
scended time because they can be summarized in this sentence: "Love God and your neighbor, and do what you
wish!" That Paul, nevertheless, is regarded as a dualist,
as father of Christian asceticism and of a morality antagonistic to sex—at least by those who regard his interpretation of sexuality as basic and absolute truth—lies in the
fact that his teachings did contain traits of antagonism toward sex as well as noticeable elements of asceticism. If
one separates Paul's observations on sex from the bulk of

his teachings, it is easy to assume that he sought to down-grade woman and sex, and that he intended to expand antagonism to sex as generally valid.

Paul stated in his First Letter to the Corinthians, "It is well for a man not to touch a woman."[23] He did not, however, deny the role of the sex drive. On the contrary, he advocated for those who "cannot exercise self-control, they should marry."[24] By viewing marriage as a safeguard of morals,[25] Paul originated a morality that eventually abandoned the central Christian elements of freedom and love. Such a view puts men and women at the disposal of their marital partners as mere sex machines, available to each other not on the basis of true selection and desire, but as automatons of mutual satisfaction.[26]

Such a mechanical union makes it impossible to establish, within the sexual area, a genuine "I-*Thou*" relationship, to use a concept established by Martin Buber.[27] In fact, Paul's views were later interpreted as a sort of marital "I-*It*" relationship degrading and enslaving the partner into a de-humanized "It." Such a relationship was, in fact, regarded as more appropriate to a sexual union before, or concurrent with, marriage than the "I-Thou" relation which implies affection or love. Citing Paul's remark that someone who remains unmarried is "better" than he who does marry,[28] moralists of all Churches established positive and negative rules based on antagonism to sex. This was tantamount to making sexuality, as such, a sin. The sex act in marriage, viewed as a necessary evil, was thus seen as the only permissible sexual activity.

These moralists ignored two important points. To begin with, Paul's teachings on sex were filled with contradictions because he was simultaneously Jew and Christian; he also was "Greek" in the sense that he used the Greek language. As a Jew, he had to approve sexuality; as a

Christian, he wished to free man from all compulsions; as a "Greek,"[29] he could not resist Dualism. The contradictions within Paul's teaching become clear where he speaks, for instance, of women. At one point he says that in Christ Jesus everyone—man and woman—are as "one";[30] then again he maintains that "the head of the woman is her husband,"[31] that man is "the image and glory of God,"[32] while "woman is the glory of man."[33] The moralists ignore that Paul did not seek to create applicable teachings, much less laws. He said specifically, in the First Letter to the Corinthians, that he was expressing only his own views. "I have no command of the Lord."[34] Paul eliminated all doubts about his "sex ethic" by making it entirely relative when he said that love "bears all things, believes all things, hopes all things, endures all things."[35] His appeal to freedom is summarized in his remark that "Christ has set us free."[36]

III

It is one of my theses that so-called Christian morality, which seeks to govern man's sexual behavior in detail, reflects the personal sexual frustrations, emotions and weaknesses of the men who propagated, and still propagate, this morality. This thesis cannot, however, be fully proven in the case of Paul the Apostle. While it has been asserted that Paul was epileptic, this judgment has been contradicted. Arthur Stern demonstrates convincingly that Paul was not suffering from epilepsy.[37] The sufferings of Paul, which he called a "thorn" in his "flesh"[38] are characterized by Stern[39] as a "psychosomatic illness" indicating a personality suffering from physiological disorders, neurotic and ecstatic elements. The Apostle's sufferings, his visions and his three-day experiences with blindness, point to a

mystically inclined person with little concern for everyday
affairs. Paul assumed that "time has grown very short"[40]
and "the form of this world is passing away."[41] We cannot,
therefore, regard Paul as a person whose nature and experiences might prompt him to endorse the pleasures of
someone with a marked sex drive, someone who would
view the physical aspects of life among God's rare gifts.
If Paul had experienced strong natural drives, he would
have done what he suggested for other men lacking in
"self-control"—he would have shared life with a woman.[42]

It is difficult to establish whether Paul's sexual ethics
reflected personal difficulties, emotions and sexual frustrations. No such doubt exists in the case of Augustine.[43]
This teacher in matters of sexuality to the West was incapable of discussing the subject objectively. His ideas on
sex and marriage reflected a mixture of emotions and frustrations as well as a revulsion against his own hectic past.
They were also strongly influenced by contemporary antagonisms toward sex. Augustine's inability to manage his
own sexual problems provided the basis of a theology that
decisively influenced the so-called Christian West. His theology of sexuality, which I am inclined to call genitocentric, views the phallus as independent from man's total
personality, even as his enemy.[44] Genitocentric theology,
which conflicts with Christocentric and anthropocentric
theology, has, since Augustine, stirred the imagination of
moralistic theologians who regard religion as totally opposed to sex.

Augustine at all times regarded sexuality as a powerful
enemy of religion. He could hardly imagine that religion
and sexuality might coexist. His hate-love of sexual activity was reflected in his prayer, "Give me chastity, but not
yet."[45] This ambivalence led to elimination of love for the
other sex and denial of the sexual drive. It culminated in

a Christian theology of sexual behavior that equated original sin with man's sexually oriented emotions and needs. This type of theology regards the satisfaction of human needs, in particular sexual union, as essentially sinful. Paradise is seen as a state that rules out the sex drive and its satisfaction.[46] Augustine regarded Hell as "the burning of lust." He, therefore, differentiated between the marital state and the sexual act which sanctions and supports marriage.[47] This created the theologically based concept of "Chastity within marriage," which to this day poisons the life of millions of men, women and their children through the rules governing birth-control. These rules illustrate the dehumanized nature, the dangerous sociological, political, economic and psychological results of a theology grounded in a patriarchal social order that permitted the Church to intrude on man's private life. It created a rigid morality which established a sexual ethic that eventually lowered the concepts of ethics and morality to a level of the ludicrous.

8. Church and Sex

Those who wish to live by Christ's teachings have long labored under the misapprehension that only one thing truly mattered: to be ready for the Great Day of Judgment. Nothing, it was felt, must endanger this readiness; man's soul must be kept free of all "worldly" consideration. This view demanded abandonment of all that might be regarded as "worldly," including the material-sexual—anything that smacked of the here and now, that might fall into the categories of "temptation" and "the flesh." This interpretation ignored the theology of the New Testament which was not only Christocentric but anthropocentric as well.[1]

Several non-theological factors contributed to this denial of the "worldly." Philosophical and social elements in the Early Church and in the Byzantine Church[2] emphasized aspects of Christ's teachings that led to Satanization of the "worldly," shunting aside original meanings. Within the sexual area, such non-Christian aspects as the ascetic emerged, reflecting the Dualism of the Hellenic world. Plato's ideas provided philosophical weapons for a theological position that opposed the "worldly." These trends caused dualistic concepts that have had a lasting effect on theology and Church: Soul-body, Church-world, Clergy-laity, Chastity-sexuality and others. These Dualisms replaced the theology of Cross and Resurrection that was, among other things, designed to heal existing rifts; instead, a theology evolved that created a deep and basic division between the secular and sacred areas of life.

In addition to the philosophical, social factors came into play. These included revulsion against sexual habits that were considered "immoral." There also developed a political theology which led to sanctification of the state and to secularization of clergy and Church. Many Christians responded to these trends with an attitude of withdrawal. They took refuge in a passive, otherworldly asceticism; literally, this meant an escape into the desert. A new life style, the monastic, emerged within the framework of Christianity.[3] It demanded surrender of all that was worldly or reflected worldly values; first of all, sexuality. Not only did these trends find encouragement; they were advanced as a spiritual style of existence that had theological legitimacy.[4] In the Eastern Church, this resulted in a theology antagonistic to sex, which regarded a passive, otherworldly asceticism as the highest Christian ideal. One example of this ultimate detachment from the worldly is the Greek monastery on Mount Athos,[5] which retains elements of Eastern Christianity in their purest forms. Mount Athos symbolizes the continuation of elements in Orthodox theology and Church that separate them from Western Christianity.[6]

In contrast to the West, the Churches of the East developed a position on sexuality that avoided pressures exerted by Western legalistic practices and clericalism. This situation resulted from several theological and non-theological developments. First, Orthodox theology could not be conceived through mystical insights or scholastic thoughts. It is possible to interpret the teachings of the Eastern Churches in mystical and apophatic ways, without becoming either an agnostic or giving way to mystical visions. An Orthodox theologian is able to proceed scholastically and to arrive at a systematic definition of truth: "He shall, however, avoid the conviction that these formulations are identical with the truth; unless he emphasizes that all we say within the church, what is taught and written, is a commentary on God's impact on history, something that remains inconceivable to the human mind."[7]

This freedom, inherent in the theological thought of the Eastern Church, avoids a theological mentality that might develop into narrow dogmatism, a legalistic or moralistic view that would abandon the critical functioning of theology. Other factors[8] have contributed to the Eastern Church's humane, generous and flexible position on the sexual life of its followers. Among these are: the view of man held by the Eastern Church, the position of the laity within the Church,[9] lack of a social ethic or social theology,[10] the power of the emperor and of the state within the area of the Eastern Church.[11] Certainly, these factors have often encouraged a negative development of the Orthodox Churches, of societies they influenced in the past and still influence at present.[12] Within the subject matter that concerns us, however, we cannot ignore that the Orthodox view of man favors a position toward sexuality,[13] which frees not only Eastern theology but Christian theology as a whole from the ruins of a past trapped in Dualism and asceticism. Eastern concepts were often interpreted in favor of asceticism.[14] However, as it viewed man optimistically, as a creature not totally ruined by sin, capable of self-renewal, enlightenment, self-fulfillment and even divinity.[15] Orthodox teachings provided a useful point of departure for a reconstruction of that basic synthesis that has been lost by institutionalized Christianity: religion and sexuality. I do not regard it as an accident that the Eastern Church, while oriented to a Byzantine ascetic ideal, tolerates a sexual life among the general population as well as within the majority of the Orthodox clergy that differs little from Near Eastern countries whose life style is decisively influenced by Islam.

II

Dualism, asceticism and the monastic view were victorious in the West. They created an atmosphere antagonistic to sex strongly influenced by Augustine's theology. At the same time, Western theology strengthened the Church within society; this contrasted with the East, where such passive qualities of patience, restraint, self-effacement, sacrifice and suffering were viewed theologically as sanctifying.[16] While a denial of power and activity fostered the development of a National Church in the East, Western theology bolstered the papal Church in its aspirations toward a universal role. In the East, antisocial and non-Christian factors created a passive, otherworldly Christianity; Eastern theology remained unproductive and tradition-bound. Western theologians tried to integrate Christian faith with human understanding. The West developed these thoughts through Aristotelianism[17] and scholasticism,[18] finding its nadir in the works of Thomas Aquinas.[19] Christianity achieved a tight unity through the monolithic papal position. This prompted it to assemble theological ideas into a grand total, organizing every little detail much in the manner of the Gothic cathedral.[20]

This ambitious blueprint was never translated into fact.

Instead of a Gothic cathedral, a system emerged that had only one aim: the rule of men over men. Clericalism was the unavoidable result. By this I mean, first of all, the influence of Church officials on all of society, the single individual as well as the community; and, secondly, the clergy's efforts to apply the Church's instructions strictly to all men.[21] These instructions, in the area of the sexual, at all times reflected Augustine who, as we have seen, fashioned his personal sexual frustrations, emotions and weaknesses into a binding law for all Christians. Thomas Aquinas, whose system became the official theology of the Roman Catholic Church as a result of papal decision, reactivated the teachings of Aristotle and Augustine. He attempted to mold them into a single harmonious synthesis and created an ethical system whose antisexual character is immediately apparent. This has been clarified admirably by Klaus Bernath in his work, *Anima Forma Corporis: An Inquiry into the Ontological Bases of the Anthropology of Thomas Aquinas.*[22] He documents convincingly that Aquinas' observations on sexuality differ little from those of Augustine. In his negation of the female sex, Aquinas out-does Augustine;[23] he went out of his way to convince mankind that woman is an *animal imperfectum.*[24]

The antisexual morality of the Roman Catholic Church, as fashioned by Augustine and Thomas, guides Western theology and Churchly practices to this day. Ever since the Council of Trent,[25] legalistic views have regulated man's sexual life on the assumption of total conflict between religion and sexuality. This concept may be found in all important documents of Catholicism, including the Encyclical of Leo XIII, *Arcanum,*[26] Pius XI's *Casti Connubii,*[27] and Paul VI's *Humanae Vitae.*[28] Catholic works on the subject of sexuality,[29] the role of confession,[30] writings devoted to the propagation of the faith[31]—all these convince the objective observer that the Catholic Church operates on the principle that whoever favors religion must avoid sexuality. Thus, virginity and celibacy are the ideal life styles of the *homo religiosus*. If one is incapable of being the ideal "Christ," unable to repress sexual needs, the marital state provides a way out. Put another way: sexuality equals sin; the marital sex act is the only permitted sexual activity, although, as a necessary evil, it achieves positive meaning only if its main purpose is the conception of children. Woman occupies a servant's position: She becomes an "It." Catholic "morality" considers the "I-It" relationship within marriage as quite "Christian," while regarding a true "I-You" relationship, before or simultaneously with marriage, as "sin." Tragically, not only Catholicism but Protestantism follows this "morality." There has never been a Reformation in the field of the sexual.

We can say, in summary, that all Churches perpetuate a "sexual ethic" utterly remote from the teachings of Christ. Theirs is the product of a masculine society, wracked by sexual anxieties, which needs an antisexual morality to provide religious legitimacy for its anxiety. This masculine society, which distorts the New Testament and Christ's words to justify its sexual fears, ignores the total teachings of Christ, in particular his demand, "Love your neighbor as yourself,"[32] whenever there is the need to satisfy aggression based on these frustrations. It is no accident, considering these circumstances, that so-called Christian nations compared with the non-Christian emerged as not only sexually immature but as particularly warriorlike.

9. The Satanization of Women

Foremost among the prejudices against women is the notion that woman envies man his strength, particularly his penis.[1] This concept, particularly that of penis-envy, cannot really be documented on the basis of available research. On the contrary, present data proves the very opposite: Since ancient times, man has harbored a feeling of inferiority toward the female sex. The resulting complexes have created a mask of superiority that prompted patriarchal prejudice. Men regarded women as supernatural beings in a positive as well as negative sense. They appeared to be creatures of special powers which showed themselves dramatically in such events as menstruation, pregnancy and birth. Woman's special qualities made her a particularly valuable and desirable object.

Once men began to see women as something valuable, they grew greedy and began to treat them as material things. The concept of woman as a creature of special, supernatural gifts opened two possibilities: adoration of woman as divine, or her Satanization. The history of mankind and its religions show that both alternatives have, at one time or another, been dominant. As soon as men overcame their fear of the opposite sex, they began their quest for control and dominance over it: goddesses and female servants of God disappeared; woman was removed from the area of the holy, from the temples that man controlled.

The Greeks, the Romans and the Jews were among historical peoples with definitely masculine patterns of society. They thought and acted in decidedly patriarchal terms. As a result, the social setting surrounding the early Church disdained womanhood. Women were regarded as a Thing. Their rights to exist depended on their ability to satisfy men. Myths and rites kept reminding men of a single concept: Woman means danger.

In this masculine world, Jesus Christ was exceptional. As we have seen, Christ's contact with women reflected his belief that both women and men are of divine origin, and therefore equal.[2] Christ's teachings in no way justify a disregard or slighting of the female sex. On the contrary, anyone who considers himself truly Christian can make no distinction between man and woman. By advocating equality, as well as by his personal example, Christ made his position quite clear. Still, the society of his day quickly overcame his example and returned to its established anti-feminine hostility.

St. Paul, for his part, struggled valiantly amidst Christ's teachings and the demands of his time. He acknowledged that distinctions between men and women are irrelevant as all humans are "as one in Christ Jesus."[3] But Paul was a product of his time, and so he simultaneously sided with the patriarchal viewpoint by speaking of man as the "head" of woman.[4] He thus fashioned the theological weapon that permitted the downgrading of woman below the position of man. Eventually, this pattern emerged within the Church as well as in the general social order.

Theology and Church did not continue those of Paul's teachings that called for unqualified love, nor his conviction that Christ set out to free us from the tyranny of law. Tyranny and Church jointly adopted the antifeminist attitude that succeeded Paul. They even formulated as a "Christian" view, based on hatred, the ultimate Satanization of woman.

Within the so-called Christian Western world, we discover the high point in a polarization of the sexes: identification of woman with sin. While man is generally seen as a spiritual and positive principle, woman personifies the principle of evil. East and West make little distinction on this point. The Church Fathers of Eastern and Western denominations were united in the view that woman is dangerous. While in the East Johannes Damascenus saw woman as a "stubborn mule" and "a frightening worm in the heart of man,"[5] as "a daughter of the lie" and "advance guard of hell."[6] The West knows the definition given by Tertullian that she is "the devil's gate."[7] Pettus Damiani, the eleventh-century monk of Clunia, exceeded all theologians and churchmen in his hatred of women. He used many curses to describe the female sex, among them "bait of Satan, by-product of paradise, poison in our food, source of sin, temptresses, whores of lust, sirens, chief witches" and others.[8]

We find a perfect example to verify this thesis in the manner in which the Church Fathers, and those who followed them, expressed their hatred of women. They sought to bolster the world of man by repressing sexual fears through this idea: not that we (men) fear the other sex; rather, women are wicked and dangerous, and we must therefore avoid them. The inferiority complex of men uses the Satanization of woman to transform itself into a superiority complex: If women were actually wicked and dangerous, men could emerge not only as "good" but even as "generous," because they refrain from destroying this wicked sex. This "generosity," this "goodness," uses positive masks. Women who are willing to fashion their ideas, thoughts and actions to suit the world of men can expect to be treated by it with "love," particularly if this society considers itself "Christian."

II

When we point out that the "goodness" of the world of men expresses itself in the fact that, although it regards the other sex as "wicked" and "dangerous" it does not destroy it, we do not mean that the Satanization and hatred of women did not lead men to an organized hunting down of women for the purpose of their destruction. The witchcraft trials, the whole whirlwind of witchcraft madness[9] provide the best evidence that hatred of woman knows no bounds. The hunting down of witches substantiates the thesis that at the moment man feels himself overpowered by fear of the opposite sex, his world develops the characteristics of homosexuality and/or a form of life antagonistic to sex altogether. In such a setting, situations are created that endanger or destroy a harmonious human existence and a normal relationship between the sexes. Into this fits the adoration of aggression, a desire for the injury and destruction of one's fellow man, as well as the egocentristic satisfaction of existing sexual needs through glorification of male genitals with sadomasochistic impulses. We have already mentioned, when discussing the headhunters, the particular role the satisfaction of these basic drives plays within a harmonious social existence.

Close examination of the world of witch-hunters shows many interesting phenomena that instantly remind us of

the head-hunters. Those mass murderers of the witch-
hunts, who in the name of the Church killed hundreds
of thousands of people in Europe,[10] are, more or less, de-
scendants of the German Dominicans Jakob Sprenger and
Heinrich Institoris,[11] who, as papal inquisitors, wrote a
pseudo-theological work The Witches' Hammer (Malleus
Maleficarum), published in Cologne in the year 1486.[12]
This volume, which has been described as "the most hor-
rifying book in world literature,"[13] differs from other
works that concern themselves with the persecution of
"heretics" in that it is solely and exclusively devoted to
the persecution and destruction of the female sex. Among
its denunciations is this phrase: "Compared to the wickedness of woman, all other wickedness is minimal."[14] The
authors suggest that, ever since Creation, wickedness has
been identified with the female sex, which is particularly
prone toward witchcraft and sorcery.

Like the head-hunters, witch-hunters Sprenger and Institoris represent a male world whose negative attitude
toward women is so strongly ingrained that they live in
purely masculine groupings that engage in vicious practices. The sadomasochistic tendencies of the witch-hunters
are as obvious as those of the head-hunters. In both cases,
a damaged relationship to sexuality is directly linked to
the aggressive actions by male groups. But as primitives
regard sexuality as natural and good, they fear women
only because the results of sex are considered dangerous;
they are satisfied to isolate women from men. The witch-
hunters, on the other hand, see themselves as representatives of a theology that satanizes sexuality as such, equates
women with sexuality, and seeks to destroy the female
sex in order to eliminate "wicked" sexuality in favor of a
man-ruled Christian world.

This Satanization of sex and women has contributed to

a tendency of the Church virtually to choke on its genito-centric theology, unable to free itself from it. This genitocentric theology showed itself clearly during the whirlwind of the witchcraft madness. It showed, among other things, that Satanization of woman does not necessarily result in the desexualization of her persecutors. The witch-hunters managed to satisfy their sexual needs, as did other celibates later on, in that they concerned themselves systematically with the genitals of their fellow men and those of the devil. The witch-hunters forced their victims into admissions that resulted in a mixture of sadistic torture and sexual excitement. Nearly all these women had to describe their sexual intercourse with the devil. Their torturers put particular emphasis on a detailed description of the devil's sexual organs. These were described as excessively big. At one time, they were described as "covered with fish scales"; at other times as "half of flesh, half of iron"; and at yet another time, as "liquid fire."[15] Paul Englisch is certainly right when he writes in his *History of Erotic Literature* that the detailed description of sexual actions was a general characteristic of sermons of the late Middle Ages.[16]

While the Satanization of women is an "ecumenical" phenomenon that weighs heavily on all Churches, witchcraft persecution remains a distinction of the West. The Eastern Churches did not participate in this outgrowth of civilization. The two inquisitors, Institoris and Sprenger, were able to perfect their hunting down of women because a Pope existed who facilitated their task. In 1484, Pope Innocent VIII issued his famous *Encyclical Summis desiderantes,* which has been correctly described as the "Witchcraft Bull."[17] The document specifically backed the work of the two "beloved sons," Institoris and Sprenger. By aiding the mass murderers Institoris and Sprenger,

Pope Innocent, through the power of his position, proved
that Satanization of sexuality and women could damage
religion generally and Christianity in particular. The document removed theology and Church from Christ, limiting
them to a male world unable to establish that "New Creation,"[18] which the life, teachings and sacrifice of Christ
had been designed to bring about.

III

But even where theology and Church did not satanize
woman but adored her as holy, a downgrading of sex is
encountered, which is directly linked to a debasing of
woman. This is shown best in the cult of Mary, which denies the sexual and the feminine in two ways: first,
through its emphasis on virginity in contrast to sexuality;
and second, through its one-sided orientation of the ideal
woman toward motherhood. Consequently, theology and
Church have seesawed between two concepts of women.
Either woman as symbol of sin is satanized and perse-
cuted, or, her existence is tolerated in male society only
because the female sex is able to create children for man
and nation.

These concepts, in the day-to-day workings of the Christian West that is responsive to the teachings of the
Churches, visualize a society where there are only mothers or whores. Mother and whore have, however, one
thing in common: They are a means to an end; they exist
to serve man. There is no room within the framework of
Christian theology for woman as an independent being,
free to decide her life, including her sex life, on the basis
of her own desire or lack of desire. Under these conditions,
the words of Pope Pius XI, directed against a "false freedom" and "unnatural equality" of man and woman, sound

like pure irony. "This false freedom and unnatural equality with man," wrote the Pope, "will lead to deterioration of woman, for once she steps down from the pinnacle and throne to which she has been lifted within the family through the Evangelium, she will soon (possibly less outwardly but certainly in reality) be pushed back into a slave position and become, as within pagan societies, a mere tool of man."[19] Let us compare this to the trivial reality that, to this day, in the German town of Jügesheim, near Offenbach, a man's death is announced by the ringing of a large church bell, whereas the death of a woman is sounded only by a small bell.[20]

10. Celibacy

I

The struggle between religion and sexuality reaches its ultimate conflict in the concept of celibacy. The viewpoint that a priest should not marry reveals the conviction that sex, including marriage, makes man so impure that he is unable to serve God.[1] This view is not new; it can be found in the Old Testament. However, those who use the Old Testament to justify celibacy ignore the fact that Judaism affirmed sexual enjoyment, and that the Jewish servants of God had to be married.[2] The contrast between "pure" and "impure" in Jewish ritual belongs to the realm of the magical, for which there is no room in Christianity.

The history of religion provides many examples which show that the service of God and sexuality are not mutually exclusive and may even supplement each other. Elsewhere in this volume, I have analyzed so-called "temple prostitution." But there are other factors to support the view that a priest should not be removed from a normal life setting if he is to serve the divine effectively; that a sexual life may well be enjoyed by someone who serves his God. Aside from marriage by clergymen or celibacy, there are other traditional ways in which a priest may enjoy full sexual freedom. A great number of mixed patterns exist, ranging from the priestess-"whore," who engages in sexual surrender as a religious act, to the priestess-virgin, as known in Roman times when vestal virgins performed their services.

There are, for instance, cases where the priest communicated the power of the Godhead to women through the sexual act; or the function of the priest-deflowerer who prepares young women for marriage by removing their virginity.[3] The sexual life of the clergy could, of course, unfold fully and freely only within religions that did not regard the deity as sexless or antagonistic to sex. Babylon and Egypt provide interesting examples of harmony between religion and sex, as well as possible unity between the divine and the sexual act, between Temple and servants, and the sexual activity of humanity generally.

In Babylon, the Temple of Bel was formed by eight levels, one on top of the other. At the highest tower stood a central altar, beautifully furnished with curtains and pillows and a large bed next to a golden table. No pictures were displayed in this Temple. No human being ever spent a night there, except for one woman who, according to the priest, had been chosen among all women of Babylon for this event. The priest maintained that the Deity visited the Temple at night and slept in the big bed. The woman chosen by the God could have no contact with any mortal being.[4] At Thebes, in ancient Egypt, one woman slept in the Temple of Amon as marriage partner of the Deity. Traditional texts often refer to her as the "divine marriage partner." Often she was none other than the Queen of Egypt herself.[5]

The Egyptians believed that their rulers had been conceived by the God Amon, who at times took on the appearance of the ruling king and in this disguise had intercourse with the queen.[6] In addition to priests, the gods of Egypt were served by a staff of priestesses known as the "song-stresses of the God."[7] Those who served Amon were numerous. Ladies of the best families were proud to belong to this circle. As the arts that pleased the Deity were identical to those used by members of a harem who entertained their master, these women were regarded as the Harem of the God. Just as in the harem of an earthly ruler, not all women were on the same level. Members of Amon's harem fell into different categories: at the top was the most respected of these women, usually the wife of the High Priest, but above all women stood a member of the royal family who was considered to be the actual wife of the God.[8]

II

Such cases, taken from numerous examples in world religion, prove that service of God and sexuality can be linked harmoniously. This is feasible as long as male society does not remove woman from the temple by identifying her with evil and the devil. If one views woman as wicked and impure, two solutions are possible. One either tries, as in Judaism, to neutralize the dangerous and impure elements of the female sex by magically oriented means, while supporting the sexual act and related carnal pleasures, or one identifies woman with sex and turns against both—woman and sexuality—as enemies of the Divine and therefore barred from the functions of a servant of God.

Within Christianity, particularly its Western segment, other factors have been added to the satanized woman and the sexual. Social elements contributed to an élite-consciousness which, as we have seen previously,[9] convinced certain male circles that they represented something better than "womenfolk" or "common people," a sexual attitude that led to homosexuality and/or celibacy. Such élite-consciousness developed particularly within Western clerical circles. Daily celebration of the Eucharist, common in several centers of the Western Church until the end of the fourth century,[10] dramatized this position. As institutionalized Christianity saw sexual intercourse as something that made a man impure, those who celebrated the Holy Sacrament daily had to separate themselves totally from human sexuality.[11]

The sexual antagonism of theologians and the Church was, however, never particularly influential within clerical marriage or in the sexual practices of the clergy. Christian leaders who tried to turn their opposition to clerical marriage into a general law of chastity were only partly successful. While in the West, up to the twelfth century, no binding and unified rule concerning celibacy governed all of the Latin Church,[12] the Eastern Church never had an enforceable law against clerical marriage. In the Eastern countries, clerical marriage remained an acknowledged fact, despite all efforts to achieve celibacy on the part of priests. The only limitation was that marriage could not be undertaken after gaining the priestly blessings. There actually exist Christian rulings, both positive and negative, that tend to protect clerical marriage.[13]

The enforcement of compulsive celibacy on all clergy, not only in the West, where the priest achieved a position of ruler over the laity,[14] dramatizes its most important aim: to separate the priest from the rest of humanity.[15] Thus, celibacy is one of many external symbols designed to clarify the clergy's special position within society. Élite-consciousness is doubly strengthened by celibacy. First of all, by its rejection of "womenfolk," it clearly separates

the priest from the "common masses." The impurity of
everything sexual, the basic argument that leads to enforced celibacy, thus moves to a secondary position, particularly as there is ample proof that celibates rarely
rejected sexual pleasures.

This should not be regarded as a moral judgment. On
the contrary, the fact that in the East[16] as well as the
West[17] the clergy did not take celibacy seriously, does
not reduce the element of the spiritual. According to our
thesis, it shows that one may be deeply religious without
renouncing sexual needs. To put it another way: The often quite intensive sexual life of popes, cardinals and
other clergy does not reflect antagonism to religion, but
a practical closing of the rift between religion and sex,
which Christian pagan elements had at one time created.

The immorality of these churchmen did not lie in their
acts but in the words they used to perpetuate a sexual
ethic, which ran counter to their personal convictions and
had nothing to do with the ethics of Christianity. This,
of course, was hypocrisy. These men perpetuated a mentality, within theology and Church, that permitted them
to say one thing, mean another, and do a third. In the
case of celibacy, this not only harmed the Church, but
also Christianity, generally, and all of society, irrevocably.[18] Celibacy is equally damaging to Church, Christianity and society. While Protestantism, by bringing back
clerical marriage in the West, turned the rectory into a
"producer" of men of higher education, Catholicism acted
as a "consumer" who absorbs many excellent energies
from the family without replenishing them.[19]

III

We must mention two additional motives for chastity:
the motive of sacrifice, and the wish of the clergy to re-

main free of all responsibilities that marriage and family create in order to concentrate on purely spiritual matters away from day-to-day concerns. In neither case is this a negation of sex. First, a sacrifice, designed to achieve a positive response, is offered the divinity. Quite aside from the fact that this tit-for-tat mentality must be regarded as un-Christian, one cannot really sacrifice something that is neither good nor desirable. Actually, the sacrifice motive, in the case of celibacy, confirms the special value of sex. Second, it is not sexuality and its related pleasures but marriage and family that stand in the way of complete service to the Divine. For this reason, there have been cases where clergy on all levels of celibacy practiced sexual intercourse but denied themselves a legitimate wife and legitimate children.

We should note that passages of the New Testament that are often cited to justify chastity prove the very opposite of what the spokesmen for celibacy advocate. The passages from Matthew[20] and from the First Epistle to the Corinthians,[21] which allegedly form the basis for clerical celibacy, either conclude "he that is able to receive it, let him receive it" (as in Matthew), or "I say this by way of concession, *not of command*" (as in Paul).[22] These two biblical sources concerning sacerdotal celibacy, assuming it is at all justifiable from biblical data, emphasize freedom of choice.

Although the New Testament, and particularly Christ and his teachings, support the arguments of the opponents rather than those of the spokesmen for compulsory celibacy, theology and Church maintain that celibacy originates in the Bible.[23] Pope Paul VI strengthened the commitment to celibacy in 1967[24] when he said, "We maintain that the present command of celibacy must even now remain linked with priestly duties; it must provide the priest with a support for his decision to devote him-

self fully, forever, singly and alone to the love of Christ,
so that his total function may be devoted to the honor of
God and the well-being of the Church. The command of
celibacy must act as a sign for the position and role
of the priest within the community of believers as well as
in all of the worldly community."[25] He also said, "Christ,
the Father's only Son, stands between the Father and
mankind, because he became man and thus mediator between Heaven and Earth. In full accordance with this
task, Christ remained throughout his life in a state of
chastity; this fact illustrates his complete devotion to the
service of God and mankind. This close link between virginity and priesthood that we find in Christ is transmitted
to those to whom it is given to take part in the dignity
and task of the mediator and eternal priest. This partici-
pation is the more complete, the more independent, the
servant of the Divine remains from all links with flesh
and blood."[26] The pagan Dualism of spirit and flesh,
which has burdened Christianity for centuries, could
hardly have been phrased more succinctly.

III SEXUALITY AGAINST RELIGION

11. The Reformation Did Not Take Place

I

One of the most disastrous developments in the so-called
Christian West was, it seems to me, Augustine's viewpoint, based on his monastic ideal and sexual anxiety, as
expressed by Thomas Aquinas.[1] Augustine projected his
own personal frustrations upon the world around him,
and this is the origin of Aquinas' outlook on life. His view
of sexuality, with its lasting influence on theological
thought and clerical practice, has outlived all attempts at
reformation. It is quite true that the Reformation which
Martin Luther[2] began was based on his own concepts of
a revision and renewal of theology and Church. He took
the position that God does not want anyone to command
the individual's soul; that man alone is saved by mercy
and faith;[3] and that Holy Scripture[4] should be regarded
as the only valid authority. Yet, Luther was unable to liberate himself from his own past; his early monastic life[5]
did not permit him to accept sexuality as one of God's
gifts. As a result, the Reformation failed to heal the rift
between religion and sexuality; in this respect, it simply
never took place.[6] The Dualism of spirit-body and
religion-sexuality formed theological thought and clerical

practice in Luther's Wittenberg and Calvin's Geneva just as it had in Rome.[7]

As in the case of Augustine, Luther's personal experiences influenced his attitude toward sex. As a monk, Luther lived in celibacy. He was neither notably vital nor vibrant, but daily encountered hypocrisy among clergy and monks who spoke of chastity and continence while they enjoyed sexual pleasure as a matter of course.[8] Like Augustine, Luther was a disappointed man. But while Augustine regarded the "world" as the cause of his disappointment, Luther saw his disappointment in avoidance of the worldly, in the monastic way of life. Thus, while Augustine wanted to get away from sexuality, having earlier led a very intensive sex life, Luther's outgoing nature demanded satisfaction of sexual needs. Augustine hoped to find a solution for his problems in the monastic life, continence and chastity; Luther sought a legitimate way to satisfy his sexual needs in good conscience.

Augustine and Luther clearly objectivized their personal sexual problems. Augustine would have liked to force all Christians to live, as he decided to do, in chastity; Luther sought to convince his fellow men that marriage, the life style he had chosen, was the only correct one. Neither Luther nor Augustine was able to overcome his past. Luther was not only heir to monastic ideals, but also to those established earlier by Augustine. That is why Luther's affirmation of marriage was, in effect, capitulation to the sex drive but not a positive recognition of sexuality as an aspect of human development. Luther the Protestant retained the convictions of Luther the Catholic that sex is a necessary evil. That is why he believed "no marital duty can be discharged without sin"[9] and that is why he described marriage as an "emergency hospital for the illness of human drives."[10] Luther believed that man is damned to engage in coitus.

Luther and the Reformers further deepened the rift between religion and sexuality through their particular view of man. In contrast to the optimistic views in the Eastern Church, which saw man as not totally ruined by sin,[11] and even in contrast to the equally optimistic view of man by Catholic theologians, Luther and his fellow Reformers saw man, and the basis of his being, as totally debased. For this reason, with sin found everywhere, the sexual part of human life cannot be free of sin. Luther's generous suggestion to "do it twice weekly," and the so-called liberal attitude of several leading Protestants toward sexuality, should not lead us to ignore the real situation. We are dealing with compromises that amount only to capitulation before the onslaught of sin.[12]

II

Calvin[13] was as convinced as Luther that sex is a necessary evil and that marriage only serves procreation and to put a leash on lust. Calvin believed that any link between man and woman "outside of marriage is cursed,"[14] that marriage is necessary, so "we do not permit lust to crash through all fences." Further, "Because of our nature, and particularly because of our desires which became unleashed by the Fall [from virtue, which led to ouster from Paradise], the marital link with women is doubly needed —except for those whom God exempts from this rule through a special act of mercy. Thus, everyone should accept what is given him! I will admit that life without marriage is not to be disdained. But some people cannot undertake it, and others can manage only for a limited time; therefore, whoever is tortured by lust of the flesh

and cannot triumph, in this struggle, must look for help
in *marriage*."[15]

Moralistic and legalistic thinking resulted from Calvin's
antagonism to sex. The word "puritanism" suffices to con-
vey the picture of Calvin's ethical impact on the so-called
Christian West. Puritanism and pietism, influenced by Luther's ethics, document the thesis that Catholic attitudes
toward sexuality were continued within Protestantism, so
that in the area of sexuality a Reformation never took
place. Calvin differs from Luther principally in that he
softened the Satanization of woman, particularly as he
revived the New Testament's concept that woman, as well
as man, was created in God's image.[16] This does not
mean, however, that Calvin advanced the equality and
emancipation of woman. On the contrary, he remained
a true product of his environment—of a male society that
separated itself from the world of women by its self-
conscious élitism. While Calvin viewed woman in a positive manner as the "helper" and "support" of man, she
was also needed to provide man with the "bodily service";
she contributes "thoughtfulness" and "tranquility," while
man furnishes "wisdom."[17]

Calvin attempted to rectify some of the things that his
predecessors among theologians and churchmen had un-
done. Luther, or the Lutheran ideal of woman, had a
negative impact on the fate of women. This took two
roads: the position of woman in society as such, and her
role as marriage partner. While Augustine decided "to
desire no woman, nor to seek her out or to marry her,"[18]
and therefore sanctioned sexual continence and chastity
as Christian virtues, Luther, for equally personal reasons,
coined the phrase, "You should engage in marriage: you
should have a wife; you should have a husband."[19] Luther regarded abstinence from marriage as unnatural but

emphasized that woman's only proper calling was to bear children and to satisfy man's sexual desire. He thereby strengthened the polarization between mother and whore which had emerged from the sexual ethic of the pre-Reformation period.

Prior to Luther, unmarried women, at least, had the right to live as nuns, independent of men. Luther metaphysically legitimized the housewifely ideal which eventually condemned woman, particularly in Germany, to restrict herself to children, kitchen and Church (the three-K mentality: Kinder, Küche, Kirche). As a result, Church circles and middle-class society view efforts toward woman's equality and emancipation with distrust. It is therefore incorrect to assume, at least in Germany,[20] that the Reformation raised the status of women as compared with conditions in the Middle Ages. Luther the Protestant, like Luther the monk, suffered from a sexual anxiety which made him incapable of reforming his environment's ideas concerning "womenfolk." Disdain for the opposite sex and the slave-nature of the married woman culminated in Luther's advice: "When the woman refuses, command the maid."[21] The Sexual Reformation has not taken place to this day because the Protestant concept of sin deepened the rift between religion and sex. This perpetuated a theological and Church-oriented society that is essentially masculine and suffers from anxiety about its own sexuality and about the opposite sex in particular. Nevertheless, the Reformation *did* change the sexual life of the so-called Christian world because it enabled people to discover that evil was identical with "self-induced" immaturity.

Through the Reformation within Western Christianity, individualism experienced totally unprecedented theological legitimacy and religious sanction. This enabled the individual to pursue his salvation, outside any collective, so that by independent thought and action he was able to seek, to find, and to realize himself. From that time on, man could hope to remove himself from evil and could pronounce himself independent from externally imposed compulsions. The liberated individual discovered at the same time that sexuality may be beautiful, natural and good. But as the synthesis of religion and sex had been totally destroyed, at the expense of sexuality, liberated man decided in favor of sexuality, but at the expense of religion, in particular at the expense of institutionalized Christianity and a Church morality antagonistic to nature.

12. Marriage

Reformation man, functioning within his newly found professional ethos,[1] sought to speak and act for himself while serving the Glory of God. He sincerely tried to improve nature and society on the basis of knowledge and rational insight. By doing this, he discovered that a good deal of what theology and Church had proclaimed as universal and ultimate truth was, in fact, remnants of a superstitious, prescientific society. Reformation man concluded that things he had accepted as part of the Divine Will, as natural or supernatural or universal, were being regarded by ethnology, sociology and the natural sciences as unnatural, even counternatural, or as phenomena dictated by cultural, social and economic circumstances.

Among these concepts was that of guilt which Augustine[2] and Aquinas had viewed as deeply rooted in sin. As sex and guilt were closely linked, sex was something to be ashamed of, forever alien to religion. Aquinas had actually even tried to explain the incest taboo by asserting that even within marriage sexuality remained linked to guilt. Therefore, he argued, one could not possibly impose marriage on someone as closely related as one's sister.[3] Aquinas was doubly mistaken. Scholars have shown that the incest taboo has very little to do with sexuality as such. Rather, it is based on quite pragmatic social and economic factors.[4] When Margaret Mead asked tribal elders what they thought of a young man who wanted to marry his sister, they replied, "What, you want to marry your sister? Are you off your head? Don't you want a brother-in-law? Don't you understand that marriage brings you two in-laws: the sister of another man, as well as the man who marries your sister? Otherwise, who will hunt with you, or help with your garden, and whom would you go and visit?"[5] If "morality" and religion played any role in this case whatever, it was certainly not in relation to sex. More likely, the incest taboo serves to widen social contacts and helps to overcome a narrowing of the group.

Thomas Aquinas was also mistaken when he linked guilt with sex and human nature. William Graham Cole states correctly in *Sex in Christianity and Psychoanalysis*[6] that "recent research concerning the behavior of children, together with anthropological reports on primitive tribes, makes the thesis increasingly unlikely that man is born with a feeling of guilt as a result of original sin or sexual desire. Among certain tribes sex is practiced without any secrecy; all sexual activity takes place in public. Contemporary kindergartens have given up the concept that small children feel ashamed by nature. Boys and girls go to the toilet and continue their talk in a relaxed fashion while emptying their bowels and bladders. Children who grow up in such an atmosphere neither show a morbid curiosity concerning the anatomy of the opposite sex, nor are they ashamed of their body functions."[7]

II

The most detrimental results within the sex life of the so-called Christian nations were caused by the so-called "truths" theologians and Church adopted from a prescientific period. Among these are the concepts that God created the institution of marriage; that God ordained lifelong monogamy; that sex exclusively serves for procreation, and that therefore any sexual activity outside of monogamous marriage, or designed for human satisfaction and not procreation, must be regarded as sinful. These "truths," which widen and deepen the rift between religion and sexuality, are still advocated as allegedly scientific aspects of sexuality. They represent lifelong monogamous marriage as a natural, universal, and timeless phenomenon.

Today, however, no serious scholar maintains that monogamy and marriage are natural phenomena that regulate sexuality; rather, they are based on cultural, social and economic conditions. Not only Marxists and Socialists[8] regard marriage as "a social institution"[9] that serves the material interests of a masculine society.[10] There is now a consensus among detached ethnologists, anthropologists, and even conservative sociologists who certainly do not advocate a "new morality" that marriage is not mainly concerned with a channeling of sexuality, or that marriage and family are institutionalization of sexual relations.[11] Of course, marriage and family must be understood as a communal arrangement, based on sex relations between man and wife. Mainly, however, the need for extended care of children is the basis for marriage and family—these as primarily economic units, socially regulated and recognized by religion and law. All stability in sex relations either originates or is substantially linked to non-sexual conditions.[12] It is sex, not marriage, that originates in nature; that is why man is, and remains, a polygamous being.

G. P. Murdock, who examined 250 primitive groups on all continents on a statistical basis,[13] encountered only forty-four cases banning sexual relations before marriage.[14] Among the societies he studied, only forty-three were monogamous.[15] Polygamy is frequent. And we must remember that a society is only regarded as polygamous where multiple marriage bestows higher social prestige than does single marriage.[16] Recent sociological research shows that, for example, in Africa south of the Sahara polygamy is a generally accepted institution, sanctioned by tradition and economic rules. In 34 per cent of these societies, the segment of polygamy extends to more than 20 per cent; and in an additional 44 per cent of these societies, it is frequent but restricted to special groups within the overall population. Among the remaining 22 per cent, polygamy exists either in very limited degrees, or not at all.[17]

Numerous missionaries have noted that the overwhelming attitude toward polygamy among African nations has not changed during the past forty or fifty years.[18] David B. Barrett writes[19] that polygamous society is not likely to disappear in the foreseeable future: "Among the 580 tribes which acknowledge it (78 per cent of all tribes south of the Sahara), we will certainly encounter strong defense of the polygamous past." Thus, Eugene Hillman[20] is certainly right in saying that the Encyclical of Pope Paul VI, addressed to the people of Africa[21] in October 1967 shows a curious lack of information and "a great deal of wishful thinking." Paul VI stated, for instance, that "particularly the system of polygamy so widely known in pre-Christian and non-Christian society, is no longer linked with the social structure and happily not in agreement with the prevailing attitude of African nations." Hillman comments: "A factual observation of the actual situation hardly justifies such an optimistic outlook."[22]

III

Monogamous marriage, lifelong union, as well as an identification of sex with marriage, are neither natural, universal nor timeless phenomena. Christians adopted monogamous marriage from their pagan environment. Theology and the Churches gained exclusive control over marriage in the eleventh century. Canonical law at that time focused on the concept of marriage as a Sacrament. Traditional teachings, up to the sixteenth century, assumed that agreement of both partners and completed coitus affirmed marriage, which thus simply legitimized the outcome of sexual union. The Council of Trent lifted marriage to the level of a Sacrament and defined it as a permanent, eternal union, ordained by God at Creation. The Council legalized and dogmatized the rift between religion and sexuality, demanding that the faithful refrain from all sexuality for at least three days before receiving Holy Communion. This implied that all sexuality results from the sensual or lustful, is sinful and should be avoided.

Theology and Church transformed the cultural, social and economically based phenomena of marriage into a universal and a "sacred" institution, which no longer had anything to do with Christ. Whenever marriage exists only because the Churches, and the nations controlled by them, demand it, a situation develops that directly contradicts the will and teachings of Christ. It begins by ignoring and doing violence to the basic truth of the Spirit of Christ that "there shall be freedom." Further, it supports the thesis that Christianity, by force of law, turned marriage into a non-Christian instrument in the dominance of men over other men.

This recalls our observation that man, whom Christ's

teaching regarded as the most valuable element, remained the single criterion from which to judge whether a value system is Christian or not. This criterion leaves no doubt that a value system which places man's sexual life under the control of an antisexual morality cannot be regarded as Christian. Morality or ethic may consider itself as Christian only when it seeks to heal man spiritually as well as bodily. Morality or ethic which creates evil is un-Christian.

The total sexual ethic of the Churches, and in particular its attempt to institutionalize sexuality in marriage while satanizing sensuality and desire for the opposite sex, has caused nothing but evil. It has led to jealousy, murder, suicide, various perversions, hypocrisy, innumerable frustrations and aggressions, total enslavement of women, the distortion of marital "sacraments" into legalized and sanctified brothels, the degradation of marital union into life imprisonment, and neglect of the most important task of marriage—the responsible care of children. These are among the results of the Churches' antisexual morality, which to this day continues its destructive work within the sexual area of human life. This morality seeks to defend itself at any price against those who, either because of religious conviction or for rational reasons, seek conciliation between religion and sex as well as the removal of the Church and its moralists from the bedrooms of society.

The rigidity with which theology and Church defend their concepts of sex and marriage reveals that they do not dare to confess, "We have been mistaken." Thus, the so-called Christian West suffers a continuing struggle of religion against sexuality. As a result, such concepts as religion, Christianity, ethics, morality, papal rule, clergy, family, loyalty and love have become degraded. Now a situation exists whereby sexuality, in order to free itself, has made religion its open and declared antagonist.

13. Prostitution

Anthropology, ethnology and sociology furnish extensive data to justify the view that marriage, while it may not be able to *control* sexual activity, does have the primary task of legitimizing the *results* of that activity. The "morality" of Western theologians and Churches transformed marriage into an insoluble, eternal union, an antidote to "sin." In doing so, it compelled the sexual partners—whether or not they loved each other—to become each other's lust objects. Marriage was degraded into a form of life imprisonment, a metaphysically sanctioned brothel. Woman was, at all times, the prime victim of "Christian" marriage which crudely degraded her into an object of lust. Aquinas states that woman loses command over her body in marriage;[1] that she is one of man's everyday needs, like food or drink;[2] that woman is, in other words, simply a means to an end.[3] That great Reformation figure Luther considered it quite proper for a man to tell a wife who rebuffed him, "If you won't, another will."[4] It comes as no surprise, therefore, that prostitution developed[5] wherever these "moralistic" notions of sex, marriage and womanhood became entrenched.

We are indebted to August Bebel, the distinguished

German theoretician of socialism, for the view that the "Christian" West entwined the enslavement of woman with the egoism of male society, monogamous marriage, prostitution and the two-faced morality of our "civilized" world. Bebel wrote in his valuable work *Die Frau und der Sozialismus* (*Woman and Socialism*)[6] that whenever man owns private property and seeks legitimacy for his heirs, he forces woman to abandon contact with other men and raises the value of virginity to its highest level. Infidelity is seen as property damage because woman is regarded as the man's private possession. Once woman has fallen to the level of property, she descends to the point where she sells herself. Bebel rightly maintains that prostitution inevitably results from woman's limited freedom within a male society that regards liberty as a purely masculine privilege. Bebel writes: "Marriage represents one side of sexual life in bourgeois society, prostitution the other. Marriage and prostitution are two sides of the same coin. A member of male society who does not find satisfaction in marriage looks for it in prostitution. Anyone in male society who refrains from marriage tends to turn toward prostitution. Men who, for one reason or another, do not choose marriage or find it unsatisfactory, find satisfaction of their sexual needs much easier than do women. Male society has always regarded prostitution as its very own privilege. But it judges harshly any woman who is not a prostitute but who steps out of line. Such judgment ignores the fact that woman has desires identical to those of man, and that these may be particularly strong during certain periods of her life."[7]

The male outlook described by Bebel, with its two-faced morality and resulting brutalization of sex, is most often encountered in strongly patriarchal societies. This is particularly the case in the so-called Christian West, where monogamous marriage, virginity and the enslavement of woman are regarded as God's will and in accord with natural law.

The antisexual battle of theology and Church has been a deciding factor wherever prostitution functioned within a European civilization, where "Christian" morality was dominant. Certainly, the number of prostitutes within a given society corresponded to the vigor with which "morality" was enforced by theology and Church. Prostitution retreats to the same degree that a society frees itself from the hypocrisy of the Christian West and its antisexual and unnatural concepts. Man's sexuality is rehumanized the further religion withdraws from the sexual. Wherever religion endorses the sexual, sexuality contributes to man's humanization. It is significant that the sexual freedom of African societies rules out European-type prostitution based on the purchase of services. It can, however, be found in territories where colonialism has led to industrial development.[8]

A recent world history of sexuality shows that prostitution and Christian morality have in the past acted in collusion with business. The author states: "In certain regions, the Church handles this matter itself. In the papal city of Avignon, Queen Jeanne of Naples acted as protector to a public brothel, the Abbaye. The women employed there were pledged to respect the hours of prayer and not to miss any of the scheduled Church events. Although they belonged to a condemned profession, they were to remain good Christians. Religious restrictions applied to customers as well: Only Christians were permitted to visit the establishment; pagans and Jews were expressly banned. The place appears to have done well; the Renaissance Pope, Julius II, established a similar house in Rome. The Church refrained from direct involvement

with such establishments elsewhere, but it was not rare
to find brothels in buildings owned by clergymen or by
the mothers superior of nunneries. It was said of one
Archbishop of Mainz, a most scholarly man, that there
were as many prostitutes in the house he owned as there
were books in his library. One English Cardinal bought a
house that was occupied by a brothel but did not close
it down. The brothel operators liked to operate under
the roofs of such owners, because it protected them from
accusations that they had dealings with the devil."[9] Karl
Saller noted that in Rome, where Pope Julius II operated
a public brothel, prostitution was an important source of
income to the Curia. Saller adds: "To facilitate the financing of the Basilica, a special tax of courtesans was introduced; it led to the collection of 20,000 ducats, more than
four times of what Pope Leo X (1475–1521) was able to
collect from indulgences sold in Germany."[10]

II

It is common to differentiate between hospitable, religious and legal prostitution.[11] These categories are inappropriate. After all, prostitution represents a specific
form of extramarital intercourse for monetary gain
whereby the prostituting individual offers herself constantly and without selection, either publicly or secretly,
mainly for the purchase of intercourse or other sexual
acts.[12] The professional element is the most important
aspect of prostitution; the prostitute regards her activity
primarily as a business which enables her to offer her
wares. While prostitution is disdained by society, it regards it as a means of controlling sexual activity, before
or aside from marriage, and endorses it as protection for
"respectable" women. These elements of prostitution are

not present in so-called religious prostitution, nor in that offered to guests as a form of hospitality. I consider it correct to redefine these concepts as sexual hospitality and sexual religious services.

The Greek word *Hierodoulos* (Servant of the Sacred) correctly describes what has been identified incorrectly as the Priestess-Whore or Temple Prostitute of ancient Greece. Actually, her service should be counted among the universal religious phenomena that dramatized the original harmony between religion and sexuality, proving conclusively that such harmony could and did exist. The Hierodoulos practitioners transformed sexual surrender into a religious act. They bridged the separations between spirit and body, between erotic pleasure and the enjoyment of metaphysical experiences, as well as between desire for the opposite sex and a desire for spiritual transcendence. "The sexual act during these services provided a sacrifice designed to bring about a manifestation of the Divine; its second function, which in structure was identical with the Eucharist, enabled man to participate in the *sacrum,* in this case represented by woman; or, as a means of direct contact with godliness; in fact, to open oneself to it."[13] The Hierodoulos, in contrast to prostitutes, enjoyed considerable respect. "The public guarded them and guaranteed their inviolability. In India they were regarded as the mates of the Temple God. Everywhere, those who belonged to this sacred group included highly admired and beautiful girls. There were princesses among them. They practiced dance and music, knew how to read and write, and were guardians of divine scripture. When, after years of strict service, they desired to marry, the richest and most powerful men competed for their favor. The more intensely these girls had served the God of Love, the greater were the demands they could make on their suitors."[14]

In many places the Hierodoulos were not permitted to leave the Temple. They lived as in a cloister, but their duty was to offer themselves rather than withhold themselves. "In addition to the female priestesses, there were male ones who held themselves in readiness to serve the Love God in a sacrifice of embrace. As the *act* was regarded as a form of *prayer* and *sacrifice*, the sex of those serving the cult did not at all times have a strict relation to that of the God. Among the Hierodoulos, men might mix to serve the Love Goddess, women with priests, to honor the Goddess of Love."[15]

The Hierodoulos cult remains best proof that neither male sex nor chastity is necessary as requirements of priesthood. Priestesses were no rarity. Throughout religious history we encounter woman as priestess, clairvoyant or prophetess.[16] In dealing with our subject—religion and sexuality—the Hierodoulos function needs to be emphasized: These priestesses proved that sexual intercourse can be a divine command. The considerable spread of a secular substitute for so-called Temple prostitution—that is, of "legal" prostitution in the so-called Christian West— shows that enmity between religion and sexuality must ultimately lead to evil. To be more specific, "legal" prostitution shows that the removal of woman from the Temple led to her enslavement, to her degradation into a lust object within a male society which regarded everything— even the gods and their world—as man's property.

14. Pornography

Pornography exists only under very specific conditions and within well-defined patterns of society. Among these are: the enslavement of woman and her transformation into a lust object and marketable property; a morality antagonistic to sex which results in the Satanization of sex, those parts of the human body and objects related to sexuality; commercialization of the needs that develop from such a situation, culminating in substitute-eroticism and a socio-economic system that promises and assures the success of such commercialization. As such social factors exist in societies that conform to the standards of institutionalized Christianity, pornography is a phenomenon possible only within the framework of the so-called Christian West.

Healthy people live in a society that responds positively to nature and sex, are able to act out their sexual needs and do not have to turn to the sexual in terms of listening, talking, reading or viewing. Wherever man's relation to nature, to his body and sexual organs is natural and direct, the operation of "sexual imagery" as a medium of satisfaction is superfluous. Why, for instance, should so-called primitive Africans buy pictures of naked women when to them the naked body is something natural, unexceptional, and a matter of daily encounter?

Successful sex merchants, such as the German businesswoman Beate Uhse, who make millions by selling sexual imagery,[1] believe that the more Catholic people are, the more they are inclined to buy pornographic materials.[2] This supports the observation that neither religion nor sexuality gains from the struggle between them, but only the darker forces within society that live on the brutalization and dehumanization of mankind. When woman was removed from the Temple and sacred society, masculine society created its own male culture whose major characteristics are brutality, aggression and the enslavement of women; within this male-oriented civilization she had to play the role of birth and sex machine. Pornography and prostitution are direct results of a culture that made possible and attractive a trading in woman as a salable product and lust object.

The difference between prostitution and pornography lies in the fact that prostitution requires only sexual anxiety and the degradation and enslavement of women, while pornography arises specifically when, in addition to fear of the opposite sex, there exists a generalized anxiety concerning all sexuality. While brothels offer men an erotic substitute, which they are unable to find in a woman as an equal and valuable partner, pornography creates substitute-erotica that are needed wherever man is unable or does not want to do anything with the opposite sex. I have elsewhere referred to motion pictures that commercialize sexual imagery as "brothels for voyeurs,"[3] in order to emphasize that, although prostitution and pornography show many similarities, they are quite different and may appear separate and independent of each other.

II

Ancient Greece provides a classic example. Even though prostitution may flourish wherever patriarchal prejudices favor the dual morality of masculine societies, the depiction of primary and secondary sexual characteristics do not fall into the category of pornography as long as they are experienced by people whose morality favors sex and nature and to whom, therefore, illustrations and descriptions of sexual actions and sexual subject matter do not seem revolting or obscene. Obscenity is based on a downgrading of the body in favor of spirituality, on Satanization of the sexual and of woman as the representation of lust; it is, therefore, only possible in the Christian West.

The word *pornography* is Greek; it actually means "whore writing,"[4] referring to a particular type of literature written either for whores, by whores or about whores, and not necessarily obscene. A pornography[5] of repelling sexuality[6] did not exist in ancient Greece. It could not possibly have developed there as its manifold representations of sexual happenings and subject matter were not regarded as objectionable or obscene and were even closely linked to religious beliefs. As we noted elsewhere in this book,[7] "obscenity" was unthinkable in a society such as that of ancient Greece. After all, it was this civilization that created holy places and statues whose function was the adoration of a goddess by the name of *Aphrodite Kallipygos,* the goddess with the beautiful backside.[8]

The development of the adoration of Kallipygos illustrates how peacefully religion and sexuality may coexist wherever men are not ashamed of their naked bodies.

Thus Athenaeus wrote: "A country man had two beautiful daughters, who quarreled over which one of them had the more beautiful backside. In order to come to a decision, they climbed a hill. As a young man happened to be passing, they showed themselves to him. He looked them over and decided in favor of the older one. He fell in love with her and when he returned to town he became ill with desire and told the story to his younger brother. The brother went into the countryside, found the young women and fell in love with the younger one. The father of the two young men, although he had wanted wealthier daughters-in-law, was forced to give in to his sons. Their fellow citizens called the two women Kallipygoi." Kerkidas of Megalopolis wrote in his verses: "There once in Syracuse, was a Kallipic pair." As these girls had come into much money through their marriages, they built a Temple to Aphrodite; they called the goddess Kallipygos, as documented in the verses of Archelaos.[9] In the letters of Alkiphron[10] we find a similar but more detailed story concerning the contest between two girls with these special features. Other literature repeats this theme in several instances.[11]

In dealing with the culture of ancient Greece, to whom we are indebted for the term "pornography," we must keep in mind that it regarded the sexual parts of man as divine objects. Antagonism toward sex in our bourgeois society, which regards as obscene and objectionable whatever relates to man's sexuality, made pornography part of a deterioration of mankind, culminating in the contrast between religion and sexuality as a disastrous break between ideal and reality. "Ideal" is, in this case, equivalent to unnatural, whereas "reality" relegates sexuality into the area of the satanic, the wicked, the sinful and the dirty.

III

As the distortion of sexual action and sex-related subject matter into pornography depends on man's subjective attitude toward nature, body, woman and sexuality, it seems impossible to differentiate between art and pornography. The perverted voyeur regards everything that is sex-related as a lust object, whether he admires the naked body of Aphrodite in a museum or whether he sees a pornographic movie. On the other hand, anyone who takes a natural attitude toward sexuality, will differentiate only between sexual representations done in good or in bad taste. He considers obscene a society and morality that seek to suppress the reproduction or description of sex-related matters, while it considers the display of crime and brutality as quite acceptable. He furthermore regards as obscene the commercialization of the sexual, notably the enslavement, alienation and exploitation of women.

The successful merchants of sex are mainly voyeurs,[12] people who cannot enjoy sex for "moral" reasons, and who turn their attention to the sexual life of their fellow man, notably youth. This is reflected in the headlines of tabloid newspapers, in the titles of pornographic motion pictures and other merchandise that exploits hypocrisy and shock value. All of them satanize sexual activity and "moralize" in a manner that provides the respectable reader or viewer with an alibi for two enjoyable hours in a porno movie.

Whoever is potent and young today seeks to circumvent the break between theory and practice. Wasting as few words as possible on his sex life, he seeks to live it as naturally as possible, although this does not bring any money into the erotica business. The merchants of erotica find their market among the impotent who, either for hypocritical reasons or for serious reasons of faith, remain loyal to churchly concepts of morality—these are people who live in the shadow of missed opportunities, filled with regret not to have lived as youth lives today. It is this sexual envy that furnishes recruits for open or hidden pornography in such heavily eroticized products as magazines, tabloid publications or films.

Our time differs from earlier periods in that the sex business used to be an erotic experience (prostitution), whereas today's commercialization deals with the sex life of others (pornography). This is the erotica of eyes and ears; its main characteristic is the inability of its supporters to free themselves from collective neuroses and psychoses that poison a practicing erotic life. Whereas earlier a so-called immorality functioned to support the sex business, today's "bedroom morality" has become its main pillar. The fact that the word "sin" has become a favorite in certain types of advertising, leading to corruption of the word, proves that bedroom morality and the related rules have nothing to do with ethics but have become a business in morality.

When I arrive at the conclusion that the commercialization of sex is not based on the "immoral" but on the "moral," I refer to the tremendous success of hidden pornography that is able to triumph because it uses the excuse of moral superiority to relate details concerning the sex life of others while labeling them as objectionable and obscene; this makes them a more salable property. This explains three important phenomena. First, protest and outcries against pornography, including fear that it might eventually become permitted (primarily based on the anxiety that the admission of pornography might destroy the myth of the "Christian" West and the results of "Christian" morality). This suggests that the best customers of the pornography enterprises are the very guardians and supporters of "Christian morality."[13] Second, advertising of a book, a film, a magazine or other hidden pornography may be praised as a "whirlwind of unleashed passions" that might dismay all "right-thinking people." Advertising of this sort is designed to arouse the curiosity and lust among those who find satisfaction in the sexual activity and perversion of others. Third, this explains why the merchandising of woman as property, within the framework of commercially created sexuality in the "Christian West," has reached an unprecedented level of success.

15. The So-called Sexual Revolution

The striking success of commerical sex exploitation has nothing to do with men's essential sexuality or with the alleged sexualization of society.[1] This can be documented by examining a three-part hypothesis. First, Western society, limited both in time and space as it emerged after World War II, is no more sexualized than earlier or other present societies. Second, what separates our society from its predecessors is not sexualization but commercial exploitation of sex based on the belief or superstition that business cannot survive without the erotic. This has created a type of eroticism that owes its existence not to sexual *experience* but to a *display* of erotica. Third, the support for sexual exploitation, and the related complication of sex life, does not come from so-called *immorality*, which would bolster the prejudices against present-day sexualization; rather, it has its roots in so-called *morality*, which equates ethics with the sex life of the men and women around us.[2]

Examination of pornography shows that at least part of our hypothesis must be correct. The "bedroom morality" of which I speak, provides fuel for the conviction of businessmen that they can't operate profitably without sex, and that the sex life and attitude of their fellow men provides them with a lucrative source of profit. As such morality satanizes nudity, while permitting seminudity, it creates a basis for business success by advertising the forbidden. Businessmen now offer so much sex that resulting moral indignation increases the curiosity and lust of the voyeurs, making other product advertisements by these same exploiters superfluous. Advertising shows that the alleged sexualization of society is actually an eye-and-ear sexuality. The naked or half-nude woman who smokes a certain brand of cigarette, sips a specific type of drink or sits on the hood of a car, meets the existing sexual needs of masculine society; yet, her presence does not satisfy these needs. The man who sees this woman is only permitted to desire her in relation to specific brands of cigarettes, drinks or cars. Only if he can afford these industrial products, and only because of his material "success," is he permitted to possess such women who, in accordance with our society's prejudices, are sufficiently "evil" and "immoral" to be "available" to whoever commands the appropriate price.

We are dealing here with the debasing of women into the role of advertisement decoy, not with a "sexual revolution"[3] but actually a distortion of both concepts—"sexuality" and "revolution." We are, after all, not dealing with sexual experience or with any revolutionary changes in the sexual practices of male society. Advertising discovered that lack of sexual experience increases the need for eye-and-ear erotica and decided to exploit woman whom it had previously transformed into merchandise for its own purposes. Thus, this alleged sexual revolution is merely an expanded commercialization of sex, powered by industrialization and the rapid development of communications media. Neither the abuse of women nor the related exploitation of sex is essentially new. Both are firmly established within the "civilization" of the Christian West, a direct result of the rift between religion and sexuality that characterizes this civilization. As the Christian West never passed through a period of Reformation in the sexual area, much less a revolution, the exploitation of women and commercialized sex have both been absorbed into industrial society. The overinvolvement with sex in our "civilized Christian society" is just as hostile to sex and nature as is the "morality" that unleashed this new wave.

II

Only once could a truly "sexual revolution" be observed: when early Christianity turned against the sexual practices of pagans[4]—who were hostile to nature—and fought them as opposing the teachings of Christ. The first Christians, who regarded the habits of their surroundings as "pagan" and denounced them as hostile to nature and sex, actually prepared the victorious march of Dualism, although this particular phenomenon was distinctly pagan. The Christians who confused sexuality with paganism ignored two important factors. First, sexuality is a universal human phenomenon and any attack on it is an attack on nature. Second, Dualism was actually a pagan concept in contradiction to divine order. The "revolution" I have in mind rests on the fact that the concept of antinature, a specific idea of paganism, was transformed into a universally applicable concept of Christianity linked with a Satanization of the natural order, mainly sexuality, which was regarded as part of the non-Christian and pre-Christian world and therefore as an enemy of the new Christian religion.

This revolution covered three levels: sexual, religious

and social. For the first time in history, man had to accept a morality hostile to nature and sex. His sex life was to be governed according to the views of a masculine minority, monks and unmarried priests with low sex drives. For the first time in history, men of strong natural drives had to accept the orders of a minority that had transformed its own negativism, impotence and other frustrations into God's will. It created a quarantine for all sex-related matters and actions, placing them in an area of sin and evil.

The revolutionary element could be found in the fact that for the first time in religious history followers of a universal faith had to choose between religion and sexuality. Whoever decided for religion had, in turn, to hate the sexual. As woman was the epitome of lust, whoever chose religion had to hate women as much as sex. Whether we are dealing with Catholic, Orthodox or Protestant theologians or churchmen, we find that their sexual ethics and morals are the concepts of Thomas Aquinas: male society is endangered by sexuality, and this danger emanates from woman who tempts man into sin.[5] Institutionalized Christianity maintains, although Christ sought to eliminate all contradictions and compulsions, the traditions of pagan philosophers and cults who negated or satanized the human body, in particular all that is sexual. All moralists who call themselves "Christian" insist that a complete Christian existence must include disdain for sexual desire, its elimination and, if possible, the separation of men from women, those arch-enemies of Christian fulfillment.

The revolution with which I am concerned manifested itself in an unprecedented separation of legal (marital) and illegal (extramarital) sexual acts. This revolution had disastrous results during the development of all societies that oriented themselves toward "Christian civilization." This division results from a split of sexuality into a relatively "proper" form of sexual activity, whose positive character lies in procreation and "evil" sexual desire, whose main aim is the satisfaction of sexual needs. The metaphysical and legal backing this division enjoyed, encouraged certain accepted attitudes, such as the notion that sexual intercourse may be generally evil but loses its negative characteristics during a wedding night blessed by state and Church. The moral theologians and lawgivers do not care whether during this night the woman may experience the first rape of her life; they are exclusively concerned with the Christian concept of monogamy; marriage without love may be a Sacrament, but love without marriage must always be a sin of unimaginable proportions.

This means, however, that people in the so-called Christian world cannot have truly natural, normal and happy sexual experiences, but experience a constant suppression of sexual desire. Institutionalized Christianity added to this condition by its acceptance of a pagan Dualism that separated the sex act and the act of procreation, condemning the sex act in favor of conception. While the sex act was, at all times, regarded as a necessary evil, views of what is permitted and what is not permitted came to incorporate a religiously oriented denunciation of all that is physiological. This concept had its origin in the rift between religion and sexuality that did not exist in pre-Christian or non-Christian civilizations. Present-day society, despite its pluralistic character, still contains remnants of such a sexual morality, based on the narrow views of a group of men who have become the binding principles of our Christian world.

Basically, then, there has only been one sexual revolution in human history: when a small group of men used the name of Christ to transform concepts antagonistic to nature and sex—part of a limited, pagan, masculine circle of dualistic orientation—and declared them to be the universally binding sexual morality of everyone who aspired to live within the concepts of Christian religion and ethics. Today's efforts to free mankind from a legalism and morality antagonistic to sex and nature[6] encounter the results of that early neopagan sexual revolution.

Like earlier efforts along these lines, this current struggle is marked by an antireligious attitude that has grown from the view that religion is the archenemy of sex and the certainty that its defeat or destruction will bring with it a development of sexuality that might be totally natural, free of problems and restrictions. Within bourgeois society, the governing "morality," with its antagonism to nature and sex, enjoys the support of Christian theologians and Churches who ignore what the middle class regards as bad or good in religion. This view sees religion, and Christianity in particular, as the causes of an antisexual morality, although these causes are actually antinatural and therefore anti-Christian laws, invented and imposed by theologians.

A situation thus exists that perpetuates and cements a rift between religion and sexuality. This, in turn, favors antisexual elements, in particular bourgeois morality, among its sacral and secular guardians. The struggle between sexuality and religion results in a dehumanized and brutalized sexuality, transformed into a protest against religion and religiously oriented values. These protests carry with them certain marginal developments in our pluralistic society. The moralist and all who are interested in repressing the sexual needs of their fellow men, label them as a "sexual revolution," further santanizing sexuality and thereby pushing it evermore into the area of evil.

It appears to me that, under these conditions, the single and greatest chance to overcome the Satanization of the sexual lies in youth whose sexual behavior, while different from older generations, is untroubled by the so-called sexual revolution or by today's commercialization of sex. Empirical studies among students[7] and other young people[8] prove that the sexual behavior of youth fails to justify such moralistic slogans as "total permissiveness," "unfettered sexual freedom," "communal sex" and other colorful projections of hopes and fears.[9]

In Germany, which is fairly representative of trends in the Western world, surveys undertaken in 1968, 1969 and 1970 have shown that youth has indeed moved in the direction of sexual liberation.[10] However, such liberation does not fit the caricature of a life style that many older observers imagined. The sexual attitude of young people does not justify talk of a "new morality" or "new cultural patterns."

These researches support the thesis that the merchandizing of sex, be it through prostitution[11] or pornography,[12] has been unable to make much headway among youth. Such merchandizing methods do not profit from the "immorality" of the young but from the "morality" of their fathers. Modern youth has achieved a mental posture that does not find a problem in sex, much less "sin," but a healthy activity for pleasure and tranquility. This trend may yet lead to a normalization that turns personal sex into something totally private, as long as it does not endanger the community[13] and does not pose a threat to individuals or institutions. There is reason to hope that the young generation will be able to separate the sexual from all connotations of "smut" and "evil," and thus renew its links with the religious. Any religion that can result from such a search would certainly not correspond to that created by theological moralists who have sought to transform their own frustrations and weaknesses into a morality that pretends to represent Divine will and universal moral concepts.

IV SEXUALITY AND RELIGION

16. *Humanae Vitae* and Its Critics

I

The Encyclical issued by Pope Paul VI on July 25, 1968, *Humanae Vitae*,[1] which dealt with birth control, encountered strong critical reaction. This Encyclical is of major importance to our examination of religion and sexuality. It threw new light on thoughts and problems within the Catholic Church as well as among all Christians who call themselves Catholic. It showed that Christianity and the Church continue to play important and decisive roles in contemporary society.[2] The daily press, both in the United States and Europe, dealt with the Encyclical as a major news event.

The impact of the Encyclical confirmed that theology and the Church may cause serious harm when they deal with such concepts as God, Holy Scripture, morality or ethics in a manner reminiscent of the Middle Ages. Rarely have the enemies of Christ been able to enjoy the discomfort of theology and Church as much as in their comments on this Encyclical. Jokes linking "The Pill" with Pope Paul VI and his Church damage not only Catholicism but all of Christianity.

The Christian world's reaction to the Encyclical demonstrated that Christians are well aware of contrasts between their personal attitudes and official Christian teachings. The conscience of all Christians oriented toward the Catholic Church had been eased in 1964 when Pope Paul VI promised to examine the question of birth control in detail; clearly Christian conscience found it unbearable to accept a rift between Christian teachings which, in the name of religion and Christianity, had satanized sexuality and ruled against natural practices.

But when the Encyclical *Humanae Vitae* appeared to perpetuate this rift, it became clear that those who shared the pope's responsibility for this document had failed to understand that Catholics were undergoing a fundamental change in attitude. They came to realize that, despite those who regard religion and sexuality as unavoidably antagonistic, these two forces can be linked in the most positive sense of the word. For the first time in Catholic history, the Pope and the ruling hierarchy of the Catholic Church experienced an unprecedented defeat in their ban on the Pill. Among Catholic families, the attitude turned out to be, "We don't talk about the pill; we just use it," or "Be obedient and neurotic; bow down and conceive."[3]

No one could have anticipated this revolt among Catholics. Even four or five years earlier, such opposition could not have been foreseen. The eighty-second German Catholic Day at Essen showed quite clearly,[4] in comparison with earlier meetings, that German Catholics are moving toward sexual emancipation, forming a movement against rigid Church controls that has no precedent in Catholicism.[5, 6, 7]

II

The Encyclical *Humanae Vitae* revealed the extent to which the bedroom morality practiced by the Churches now encounters increasing resistance. If the Pope had used his Encyclical to open a broad and liberal road, no one would have become quite so aware of the havoc institutionalized Christianity can wreak within the intimate spheres of man's sexual life. Many parents, prompted by publication of the Encyclical to reveal their problems in public,[8] confessed that their children had been conceived merely for religious reasons.[9] The Church's attitude toward birth control[10] dramatized its dehumanizing influence; it also revealed the negative sociological, political and economical results created by the Church's attitude,[11] as well as the psychological impact of a legalistic orientation basically antagonistic to sex.

The Encyclical *Humanae Vitae* made it clear that the Church had become the slave of its own laws, of its legalistic and moralistic framework; men who practice celibacy showed themselves incapable of understanding the problems of married men; theologians and clergymen, whose masculine society despises women, proved incapable of taking the concern of women into account; their sexual ethic and morality led to thoughtless cruelty; their "morality" and "ethic" created a disrespect for human dignity which is essentially un-Christian and anti-Christian.

A report in *Time* magazine documented this development.[12] According to the news magazine, the Vatican instituted a "secret diplomatic offensive" designed to hamper the financing and official support of birth control; at the same time, the Vatican put pressure on governments and international organizations to discourage birth control practices. The specific targets for this campaign were the United States, the United Nations and particularly the United Nations Childrens' Fund (UNICEF). Existence of a secret memorandum concerning birth control, directed to all papal representatives, was confirmed by the Vatican spokesman Allessandrini. The document provided papal representatives with data for their own information and for others who might find it useful.[13]

Other religions, such as Islam, which are just as concerned with procreation, regard birth control as an important means of fighting the population explosion and its resulting social, economic and political hardships. The Catholic Church, however, retains its traditional restrictions on birth control. While the witchcraft campaigns of the past made women their most immediate victims, the Church's "morality" makes children into victims. It would only be necessary for the Pope to read a single report on conditions in the so-called Third World to dramatize his responsibility toward children who could wish for only one thing: that they might have never been born. Millions of children, whom I would like to call "papal children" because they owe their existence to the Pope's will, live and die in hardship and poverty. That, in addition to *Humanae Vitae*, there exists the forward-looking Encyclical of Pope Paul VI, *Populorum Progressio*,[14] must go down in Church history as a unique example of cynicism.

The extent of misstatements and hypocrisy behind the rulings on birth control can be illustrated by comparing the Churches' rigid morality with their ethical principles based directly on Christ's teachings. Thus, the New Testament[15] states, "Let what you say be simply 'Yes' or 'No'; anything more than this comes from evil."[16] But just as moralists and Churches have blessed weapons and bombs, they use the name of Christ to ignore the death of millions.

Neither the will of God nor Christ prompt theologians and clergy to formulate and enforce laws antagonistic to sex. These laws only disguise their originators' desire to rule their fellow men, to create a world that accepts as objective reality, based on the will of God, the very sexual frustrations that are the daily curse of these moralists. The motives of the sex moralists have nothing whatever to do with ethics and morality, and even less with the will of Christ. They grow from an anxiety concerning sex and women and from the sexual hatred of theologians who despise sex as a life force equal to the life force of religion. As theology and Church are spokesmen for a religion of enmity to sex, which perpetuates a pagan Hellenistic Dualism, they oppose sexuality—as in *Humanae Vitae*—with the claim that possible separation of lustful sexuality and its results can be described as sinful. Theology and Church fear that successful separation of sex from its results might eliminate the best ally of their "morality": fear of venereal disease and of pregnancy. This could seriously limit their power and influence.

III

The Encyclical *Humanae Vitae* confirms that post-Council Catholicism is no less antagonistic to sex than it was before the Council. The Second Vatican Council could not or would not break out of the vicious cycle that has placed theology and Church under the influence of a morality antagonistic to sex. Thus, the chapter on marriage in the Pastoral Constitution of the World Church demands serious attention to the virtue of continence in marriage, so that "the children of the Church" may avoid birth control methods banned by teachings "in their interpretation of divine law."[17] The Council could not or would not free itself from a bedroom morality that degrades theology and Church. It remained true to Augustine's concept of marital chastity which grew out of his own unhappy relationship with the opposite sex, his personal frustrations and sexual difficulties.

The Council sought to acknowledge that "living conditions of the present time"—which simply means today's society—make it difficult for a married couple to have many children;[18] but it placed these conditions into a framework of criteria of a period that had little use for freedom, love and human rights. Post-Council theology of sexuality remained as antagonistic to sex and as inhuman—which means, un-Christian—as was Catholicism prior to the Council. *Humanae Vitae,* which emerged after the Council, plays havoc with the ideas of the Council's initiator, John XXIII, who had favored human dignity in day-to-day living, and a life style of freedom.[19]

17.   Revolt of the Priests

The revolt of laymen, following publication of the Encyclical *Humanae Vitae*, clarified two points. First, Christians who orient their thoughts and life on the teachings of the Catholic Church had become aware that whatever is not based on honest conviction is sinful.[1] Second, today's Christians have come to realize that sex and religion need not be antagonists. The same points were clarified by yet another revolt: that of the priests against clerical controls, particularly against compulsory celibacy.

Albrecht, Archbishop of Mainz, wrote in about 1540 in a letter to Nuntius Morone: "I know that all my priests have concubines. But what am I to do about it? When I forbid them to have concubines, they either want wives or they become Lutherans."[2] Catholicism after the Council forced bishops and archbishops to view the sexual problems of their priests differently from the viewpoint of 1540 and to find other solutions for them. The young generation among Catholic clergymen does not cheat, nor does it want to be cheated. It looks at it this way: If the life force of sex is strong enough to endanger the myths of clerical chastity, then theology and Church should be honest enough to admit that resistance to sex is a grave error, and that a priest should live like any normal man who may enjoy sexual satisfaction as a gift of God and nature. The priest, like any normal man, believes that sexual satisfaction should be acknowledged and sanctioned by society as well as by the Church. Today's priests do not wish to be regarded as fallen angels but as decent, good human beings. They do not want to play the role of wicked holy men but simply of good Christians. That is why they are in revolt against their bishops and archbishops.

But Pope, archbishops and bishops have made the life of the clergy so intolerable that they must either abandon all independent thought and actions or, to be able to live with themselves, give up their faith in the Church. The examples for these decisions are by now legion. It has come to a point where priests feel that their primary loyalty is expected to be to the Church rather than to Christ and his will. This system demands compulsory celibacy, one of the most cruel means by which a system can achieve total dominance over its servants. But the moment priests become aware that sin is not to be found in sex but in the hypocrisy and distortions of their betters, they discover a wider reality that leads to affirmation of the sexual and creates the basis for liberation from the ruling methods within the Church. Certainly, elimination of the rift between sex and religion has given priests a new experience of liberation which places them in closer contact with the sources of their faith in the spirit of Christ, who said "there is freedom."[3]

Headlines in the daily press are full of such news as this: "Dutch priests vote against celibacy"; "Increasing disenchantments with bishops"; "Church unity more important than celibacy"; "Theologians ask bishops for clarification of celibacy," etc. Following the Second Vatican Council, the revolt of the priests against compulsory celibacy communicated itself to the general public. This resulted from an unprecedented clerical protest against rulers of the Church who had tried to perpetuate a form of Catholicism that placed legalistic and moralistic concerns above love and freedom. This protest, a "Protest of Love," called for greater love and humanitarianism, actually for more Christianity within the Church itself.[4] In the area of the sexual, this protest meant that some priests were firmly convinced that interference with individual freedom of decision, cloaked in a "morality" that calls itself "Christian," must be evil and in ultimate conflict with Christ and his teachings.

II

This clerical protest created a feeling of solidarity among priests that was dramatized at the conference of European priests[5] at Chur, Switzerland (July 5–10, 1969). It created an international movement of priests who desired joint thought and action.[6] Concerning celibacy, a resolution adopted unanimously on July 8 by all national delegations[7] advanced the following points: Compulsory celibacy contradicts the spirit of biblical tradition because there are no pressing arguments, either in Bible or tradition, that support it. Therefore, many priests as well as candidates for the priesthood deny any obligatory connection between priesthood and celibacy. More and more priests find that the system of Church administrations forces them, if they wish to retain their positions, to engage in clandestine marriage. This contradicts the personal freedom and dignity of man and is particularly degrading to the women in question.

The priests emphasized further that the present form

of compulsory celibacy is debatable; they recognized and stated clearly that priesthood and chastity are not fundamentally linked with one another; from a Christian viewpoint, celibacy has a prophetic meaning which present-day rules tend to disguise, reducing its credibility and effectiveness; it is unjust to accuse priests who desire marriage of unfaithfulness toward their initial pledge; the argument in favor of chastity is based on the false concept of "undivided service," which contradicts all experience. Finally, celibacy is an affront to other Christian denominations and to other professions.

The clergy demanded the official removal of the element of a "compulsory celibacy" and addressed itself to the conferences of bishops and other conventions, including the synods. They called for solidarity among married and unmarried priests; guarantee of continuous employment for married priests—in consultation with local parishes—with full credits; new positions for priests, based on a free choice of life status; and the solution of the celibacy questions, not in Rome but in all of "God's People" in the territorial Churches.

The celibacy resolution, passed by European priests at Chur, should be viewed as a serious clerical effort to remove the rift between sex and religion by placing a higher value on sexuality among a group of men who occupy an élite position because, as "religious" people, they allegedly have no sexual needs. The resolution of the priests demythologized the Catholic priesthood and its alleged religion-without-sex. This had dual significance. First of all, the priests admit that to stay in office they see themselves forced to engage in "clandestine marriage." They further acknowledge that clerical "chastity" is a myth which exists only because the Church would rather tolerate hypocrisy than truth and freedom. Lastly, these clergymen leave no doubt that they regard the Satanization of women and sex, together with the downgrading of marriage in comparison with celibacy, as intolerable.[8]

III

The public protests of clergy against celibacy were accompanied by events that further exposed the myth of religion-without-sex. Public confessions by "fallen priests,"[9] as well as the numerous resignations of priests from their offices,[10] shows that religion-without-sex is tragic for many men who are victims of an image of "Christian fulfillment" that results from an unhappy mixture of Dualism, Morality and Legalism. With it go disdain for human freedom and sex as well as Satanization of women. These compulsions isolate the faithful in a masculine society that pressures the individual until he is no longer his own master. This society makes sure that any priest who opts for freedom and gets married encounters unending difficulties which may cause the emotional and physical breakdown of "fallen" priests.[11]

In order to create the impression that "wicked" sex and, even more, "wicked women" remove these "holy" men from the paradise of clerical male society, they are shown to be literally hell-bent. At the same time, priests are asked to believe that the frustrations of "fallen" priests are much greater than those of priests who retain their chastity. More and more priests have had to go against their own better judgment and submit to Church control, although this forces them to suffer the frustration of men who mean A, say B, and have to act C. Of course, such men are not useful to the Church, to society or to Christ himself.

Concrete examples show how unbearable the control system of the Catholic Church can become to clergymen; yet it also becomes clear that a synthesis of sex and religion can advance the downfall of this system. Let us

take the example of the British priest and theologian
Charles Davis who, in December 1966, announced that
he was leaving the Church to get married.[12] Davis, one
of the leading theologians of British Catholicism, enjoyed
world-wide prestige. He declared in the London *Observer* that, without his wife's help, pressures from Church
administration might have driven him into a nervous
breakdown. Without her support, he might have been
psychologically unable to break with a system to which
he had been linked by a lifetime of intense and satisfying
activity.

Davis proved still another thing: that a woman may
lead a priest, despite his removal from the Church as an
institution, closer to God and Christ. Four years after
leaving the Catholic Church, Davis gave an interview to
the British Catholic periodical *The Month* (January
1971). He said on this occasion: "My past has dogged
me to some extent. I felt it reasonable at first to answer
the request of groups and audiences to explain my position concerning the Church. But I've become increasingly
reluctant to do so. Explaining my objections to the Church
has tended to give people the impression that my own
thinking on religious questions is largely negative, and
that in fact is untrue. Apart from that, I have become tired
and bored with the debates concerning the authority of
the Church and the institutional form of the Church. As
I've just said, these issues have receded into the background of my thought. I've been much more concerned
with the basic religious questions such as our relationship
with God and the uniqueness of Christ. I have, when asked
to speak, tried to indicate that I don't want to speak concerning the Church and that I have something to say on
other questions."

18. Beyond the Dualism of Matter and Spirit

I

The concerns of priests and laymen, which we have noted in the two preceding chapters, are part of a historical effort to overcome the separation of matter and spirit. This Dualism, a result of the Catholic Church's moralistic and legalistic control system, is significant in today's efforts by priest and layman. I think it is useful to clarify these developments by dealing with the differing concepts of National Religion,[1] Universal Religion[2] and National Faith.[3] Certain basic criteria of religious thought and action need to be emphasized, as they are basic to an understanding of our main subject, religion and sexuality.[4]

The structure of National Religions is characterized by the fact that they were religions of the whole populace (as in the case of ancient Rome), not of a specific stratum of population. The element of salvation has been basic among Universal Religions; they are religions of the individual, and everyone is a pillar of the faith. The central characteristic of Universal Religions is that they concentrate not so much on salvation[5] as on limitations and that their world becomes an object of rational understanding and conscious creation. We cannot ignore, however, that Universal Religions may create a new collectivism; one may therefore speak of a continuous process that leads from collectivism to individualism and back to collectivism. Man overcame the original collectivism of National Religions but eventually surrendered to a collective unit. This final form differed from the original collective by adjusting to narrow national concepts. While the original collective speaks of National Religion, the collective that develops from a Universal Religion evolves into a National Faith.[6]

The National Faith of a whole nation, such as ancient Greece and Rome, existed as a broadly based structure, whereas within a more developed national pattern only a certain élite is the bearer of a given faith. When we speak of a National Faith, we imagine a "mass religion," whose base is an unstructured multitude that has a primitive religious pattern and feeling as its central characteristic.[7] The individual's opportunity within a "mass religion" lies in the possibility of moving away from a collective pattern. He is able to abandon a traditional milieu; if he commands personal charisma, he may even develop a new process leading from collectivism to individualism and finally to a new collectivism.[8]

Societies with a strong tradition of National Faith have a high regard for such groupings as the family. They offer a prestige pattern for the family beyond its narrow limits, including clan and tribe, which they place above the individual as well as above total society. In other words, their scale of values makes one's own group the most valuable unit.[9] This forces the individual to subordinate himself to the will of the unit, abandoning a considerable part of his independent thought and action. In such a grouping, obedience and dependence are respected characteristics. The individual must remain strongly traditional and has to react in accordance with acceptable stimuli.[10] Leadership also adheres to a traditional pattern: A leader commands obedience on the grounds that everything has always been done in a certain way and cannot possibly change.[11]

Societies whose traditions are oriented toward a Universal Religion contain seeds of dynamic change, although this does not mean that such seeds are always likely to sprout or that changes are necessarily either positive or constructive. Here the individual is the most important factor. Within this pattern, the individual as bearer of faith within the Universal Religion does not find himself in a position of automatic salvation but subject to temptation. In other words, the individual must decide what is of value;[12] it is not automatically imposed on him.

Different situations may result in various value systems.[13] Such systems may be bearers of a tradition whose stability or flexibility depend on traditional views of individual action. The individual may eliminate, encourage or control whatever befalls him. The most important tasks are ways of eliminating the experiences of evil. These are decisive in overcoming one tradition before establishing a new one.

To overcome evil, actions need to be taken that are closely related to anything experienced or recognized as evil. Within National Faiths and the traditions based on them, isolation of the individual from his group is regarded as evil. Eliminating evil is identical with membership in one's own group; forms of action are limited by total dependence on that group. Within Universal Religions, content and form of evil are decided by the individual, who seeks personal salvation independent of his group so that everyone experiences and recognizes evil in a different way.[14] Strong personalities who emerge as charismatic leaders or teachers become founders of religions and philosophical concepts because they promise salvation on the basis of specific actions.

Basically, despite the numerous systems that promise salvation, there are only three important major salvation schemes. One approach promises salvation through absolute spirituality, mysticism, contemplation, etc., which totally negate or ignore the world and its material value systems.[15] Another approach views the world as the object of rational insight and conscious creation, believing that, in addition to God's action toward salvation, individual initiative is required.[16] The third approach calls for materialistic methods[17] on the part of the individual who seeks to overcome evil. Within these three directions and their variations, all cultural and underlying value systems are grouped and reflect the different traditions of East and West.[18]

II

When matter, whether as one's own body or in material things, is basically regarded as a source of evil, the individual must struggle against all material needs and values. These are opposed by needs and values that may be described as spiritual. Where material things are the only accepted reality, it is consistent and logical that salvation, or the elimination of evil, can lie only in the satisfaction of material needs; values that hamper such satisfaction must be attacked and destroyed.

But Christ, his life, actions and teachings have shown convincingly that those who seek salvation in Christianity can find it neither in the spiritual nor in the material. The road to salvation within Christianity lies in efforts, through faith, to eliminate the cause of evil; namely, antagonism to God, to man himself, to his fellow man and to his environment. Christ spoke of the will of God, who so loved the world that he gave his only Son, "so that whoever believes in him should not perish but have eternal life."[19] God's unlimited love manifested itself in Christ crucified, eternal symbol of God's unqualified love.

Thus, the message of the Cross became God's affirmation of his total love for mankind. The Cross and Death of Christ disarmed any thought and action that might benefit from a rift between friend and foe and eliminated all doubt regarding contradictions between spirit and body, man and nature, spirit and matter. Incarnation meant reconciliation: reconciliation of God with man, of man with himself, with his fellow men and his environment. Reconciliation provides us with insight significant to our subject matter because the concepts of body and flesh are never to be regarded as antagonists to the Christian outlook. God did not make himself known through a phantom but through Christ, who lived on earth as a complete human embodiment. His bodily reality was incorporated in the Resurrection as a sign that the life, action, death and resurrection of Christ served to renew all of creation in favor of man, who himself enjoys the opportunity of achieving the completion of this renewal.

The classic phrase "God became man, so that we might become as gods"[20] liberates us from non-Christian dualistic concepts. God became man so that man, because of his faith, could free himself from all social and natural compulsions in order to create a new society and world that could correspond to a new God-like creature. With this understanding, Christology and Christian anthropology should have been able to prevent a polarization be-

tween the spiritual and the material within the so-called
Christian part of the world.

But, as we are aware,[21] a number of non-theological
and non-Christian philosophic and social factors elevated
elements antagonistic to the world, latent in Christ's
eschatological teachings, toward Satanization of the
worldly. These elements were able to leave a one-sided
imprint on early Christian belief. As a result, dualistic concepts could establish themselves firmly. They left us with
contrasts between soul and body, church and world,
clergy and laity, chastity and sexuality. This damaged a
theology of the Cross and Resurrection, which should
have eliminated just such contradictions. In particular,
the contrast between spirit and matter created a fatal
division between the sacred and the profane within our
lives. We find this in its purest form within the Eastern
Church, where salvation is sought through absolute spirituality, mysticism, contemplation, etc., together with negation of worldly and material value systems.

The unholy alliance between Church and state in the
East, as well as secularization of Catholicism in the West,
tends to neutralize several contradictions but does not
liberate man from the compulsions created by some of
these Dualisms. On the contrary, they sanctify and sanction only such secular powers, which in the name of Christ
assert that only the forces resulting from a contrast between spirit and matter can promise salvation. In other
words, the elimination of a contrast between spirit and
matter, or between sacred and profane, is only tolerated
by the Churches when it assures the rule of a "spiritual"
élite over the "common" masses. Concepts such as roy-
alty, crown, throne, state, order, obedience, rule, service,
honor and punishment are acknowledged as part of an

"order under God's will."[22] We can thus understand why Pope and clergy should have succeeded in gaining vast powers.

Prior to the Reformation, the individual was only able to escape evil by total dependence on middlemen between this world and beyond. This was doubly the case because man at that time was deeply concerned about life after death, which seemed much more important than life in this world. The Reformation attempted to change this situation radically by aiding the individual to help himself to achieve salvation, independent of the collective by personal thought and action. The resulting new theology sought to liberate man from the multiple compulsions inherited from the pagan Dualism of spirit and matter, a Dualism that had distorted Christianity, theology and the Church for centuries. But in these areas, as in the area of relations between religion and sexuality, the Reformation never took place.

The post-Reformation period revealed that a Christianity which ignores or negates man's material needs betrays Christ. Neglect by the Church of material values, and their negation in the name of Christ, forced men to seek salvation where it promised a concrete satisfaction of his needs: on this earth, and in this world. Viewed this way, materialism was a logical reaction of mature man, who became his own master through the Reformation, against the purely spiritual advocated by the Church, which was the source of certain situations of evil.

Many theologians who recognize the dangerous impact of a rift between spirit and matter prompt their Churches to revise concepts of "worldly" and material things in order to overcome the split between matter and spirit. This movement encourages developments that unite clergy and laity in common action against a churchly morality and legalism that would perpetuate the pagan Dualism of matter and spirit, as well as a "morality" antagonistic to women and sex.

19. The Positive Meaning of Asceticism

The process of overcoming the Dualism of matter and spirit, as well as elimination of the rift between religion and sex, can be observed in the emergence of a new meaning for the word *asceticism*. As we noted,[1] this concept developed into a symbol of hate against women and sexuality during the early periods of Christian and Church history.[2]

The Greek word *ascesis* had a positive meaning in ancient times when it was used in terms of bodily discipline in sports or exercise. Motives and aims were positive because asceticism meant self-control to achieve a strengthening of body and character. It had a positive meaning toward matter and the world as well. Under the influence of Dualism and the contrast between spirit and matter or soul and body, which Dualism implied, both origin and aim of *ascesis* changed. From then on, asceticism implied a negative attitude as a basis for achievement of positive spiritual aims.

To the degree that "world" and body were regarded as enemies of spirit, soul and supernatural reality, the concept of asceticism gained a negative meaning. This meaning extended into secular society, its values and its relationship toward the gods, or God. *Ascesis* was still used as referring to physical exercise; but while the ancients were free of dualistic concepts and saw self-control as a means of strengthening the body, dualistic ascetics wanted to achieve the opposite: a weakening or mortification of the body. As the sexual enjoyment implies affirmation of the body, the sexual needs of man and the role of the woman were declared to be enemies of asceticism. The dualistic concepts of the ascetics culminated in the rift between sexuality and religion. The final point of this development was *Christian asceticism* which, under the influence of Dualism, deepened the rift between religion and sex. Eventually, Christianity acknowledged only the type of ascetic whose main task was resistance to sexual needs and to the female sex. Identification of asceticism with the monastic life was a logical result. Martin Luther and the Reformation liberated asceticism from its narrow link to sexual life, giving both *ascesis* and the ascetic new and positive meanings.

II

Before we turn to the positive meaning which the Reformation gave to asceticism, let us remember our earlier examination of sexual points of view in the Old Testament and in the teachings of Jesus Christ. We regard the traditional concept of a Christian asceticism as negation and a throttling of the body as a Satanization of the sexual that cannot be justified either through biblical references or on the basis of the life and teachings of Christ. The Old Testament can obviously be characterized as non-ascetic,[3] and Christ's life was molded in such a way that his enemies could denounce him as a "glutton and a drunkard."[4] It was not Christ but the Alexandrian Jew Philo[5] who, under the strong influence of non-Christian Platonic, Pythagorean and other concepts, labeled Christian theology dualistic and ascetic. Philo, whose work combined Judaism and Hellenism at their height, advocated a radical Dualism, contrasting God and world, soul and body. He endorsed a way of life whose most notable elements were pessimism, negation of worldly values, a downgrading of the body and its requirements. The Dualism and life style he suggested were developed by the religious concept known as gnosis,[6] which in turn influenced the development and spread of Christian monasticism.

Christian asceticism and monasticism are multidimensional phenomena which, as I have noted elsewhere,[7] served the task of Christ in many ways. They are, however, not identical with it, and they have damaged Christ's aims wherever they attempted to impose their particular ideas as the generally valid concepts of all of Christendom. Above all, asceticism damaged Christ's task where it imposed the theological point that a non-marital existence is superior to marriage. Born of the dualistic idea, asceticism came to regard the sexual as an antagonist of religion, convincing Christians that they can satisfy their sexual desires only with a guilty conscience.

The damage which this Satanization of the sexual was able to do, in the name of asceticism, was relatively small within the Eastern Church. It could function in the East only as a peripheral, aimless asceticism (*passive ascesis* by monks), so that its concrete sociological effect was barely noticeable. The impact of ascetic theology, while negligible, had significance in Western society where it achieved the form of a non-worldly rational asceticism (*active ascesis* by monks). Its concrete sociological impact could be felt wherever active monks' *ascesis* was able to take place. As a result, moralistic and legalistic antagonisms to sex were more effective in the West than in the East. The destruction[8] which Christian asceticism left behind was thus greater and more dangerous in the West than in the East. While Eastern asceticism was largely an expression of devotion, or a contemplative life, it became a synonym of antagonism to sex and women in the West. There, captured by morality and by the theology that adopted it, asceticism became genitocentric.

III

Asceticism was given a new anthropocentric and Christocentric content by Luther and the Reformation.[9] There, it became desexualized. True, the sexual ethic of the reformers depended on dualistic ideas. However, the Reformation's pessimistic view of man, which perpetuated the rift between religion and sex, made the Eastern type of asceticism quite unacceptable. Luther was certain that man may achieve salvation by mercy and faith.[10] This prompted him to oppose all ascetic works, notably the concept of ascetic theology that continence may be achieved by individual determination. Luther felt that even if the monastic life were agreeable to God, the ascetic person could not by himself retain his restraint and, should he continue a cloistered life, would unavoidably commit sinful acts.[11] "Flesh and blood remain flesh and blood, and the natural tendencies and attractions have an irresistible strength, as everyone can see and feel."[12]

But Martin Luther's great achievement rests not only in the desexualization of asceticism or opposition to genitocentric asceticism, concentrated on the sexual life of the *homo religiosus;* he also achieved a declericaliza-

tion of the concept of vocation.[13] This created the basis
for a positive ascetic concept,[14] an "ascetic Protestantism,"[15] which brought Christian *ascesis* into daily life. It
"entered the market place of life, shut the monastery doors
behind it, began to bring its method into everyday existence which enabled man to function fully in the world,
although it need not be of the world or for this world."[16]

In order to describe a Christian life task, Luther quoted
Paul (I Corinthians 7:20): "Every one should remain in
the state in which he was called." This created a professional concept, "showing how important the original view
of vocation was, although today the idea of a calling has
outgrown its basic religious foundations."[17] The quarrels
of theologians and commentators do not change this fact,
although some believe Luther emphasized an appropriate
subject matter but did not use the proper biblical quota-
tion. However, it is generally acknowledged that his concept has become so widely accepted that it would be
foolish to contradict it.[18] Whether or not Luther quoted
Paul correctly, he "furnished proof that the fulfillment of
duties in the inner world is under all conditions the only
way to please God, and through it, by God's will, every
permissible vocation is equal before God."[19]

The specific sociological meaning of a vocational calling can only be fully understood in relation to the Calvinistic vocational ethic[20] and its impact on the economic
life and spirit of industrial societies.[21] The ascetic Protestant conviction that diligent vocational fulfillment is a
mark of grace and corresponds to a situation of salvation
was of decisive importance for industrial development.
The concept that asceticism and vocation are achievements that may be appropriate to anyone who wishes to
assure his ultimate salvation, provided a rationale for a
life style whose metaphysical value prompted followers

of Calvinistic vocational ethic to prove themselves in personal life as well as in social, economic and political activity.

Man thus found a new positive meaning, the ability to achieve his own religious charisma through specific actions. The most important achievement could be found in vocation and its fulfillment. Max Weber comments: "The world exists—and exists only—for this: the greater glory of God who chose Christ in order to—and only in order to—enhance the glory of God in the world through obedience to his laws. But God demands social achievement of all Christians because he wishes to see the social pattern of life correspond to his laws and to achieve his aims. The social work of Calvinists in this world is therefore only work *in maiorem gloriam Dei*. Even professional work that serves community life has this characteristic. We observe the origin of labor in neighborly love even with Luther. But with him it is an undefined, purely constructive-speculative beginning, whereas with the Calvinists it becomes a significant part within a system of ethics. Loving one's neighbor expresses itself—as it only serves the greater glory of God, not his creatures—mainly in the fulfillment of normal vocational tasks; this takes on a noticeably factual and impersonal character: it is a service in the rational creation of the social environment. The marvelously practical creation and perfection of this environment which, according to biblical revelation and rational insight, apparently serves the need of man, permits the view that service of such impersonal social usefulness adds to God's glory and is therefore God's will."[22]

When we think once more of the three types of *ascesis* —Eastern, passive and non-worldly asceticism which the world abandoned for the contemplative life; the non-worldly, rational *ascesis*, which became the active monastic *ascesis* of the West; and an inner-worldly *ascesis*, which contains a "duty"[23] imposed on the world by the religious virtuosi—we can conclude the following: While non-worldly asceticism achieves, by a negative attitude, positive outer or inner worldly religious aims, ascetic Protestantism returns positive meaning to the Greek word *ascesis* by permitting a positive attitude toward the achievement of constructive aims, both in the religious and a socioeconomic category. This can be seen in the change that one of the phrases of monastic asceticism has undergone: "Thou shalt abandon; abandon thou shalt," which may be replaced by the positive and quite worldly, "Thou shalt gain; gain thou shalt."[24]

20. Sex and Religion: Can the Rift Be Closed?

Ascetic Protestantism based its rules of conduct within this world on the anticipation of a world beyond.[1] As a result, achievements based on religious demands could be dealt with within this world and its patterns. Thus, the Christian world gained a new and positive meaning, becoming the territory on which its religious charisma could establish itself by rational achievement. The main medium of this achievement could be vocation and diligent professional fulfillment. Such asceticism can be expected of anyone who is certain of his immortality and knows that immortality or salvation is neither freely given nor channeled through an intermediary; one has to achieve it oneself. The specific sociological, economic, political and cultural impact of these ideas can be found in all democratic or pluralistic social forms.

"Pluralistic society" means a social system wherein the individual must decide daily which values[2] are in accordance with highest standards.[3] This includes the decision whether or not sexuality and religion are antagonists. Modern Christians, among them theologians, at least maintain that sexuality and religion need not necessarily be at war with each other. Therefore, the impression has gained ground that our pluralistic society makes elimination of the rift between sexuality and religion not only possible but has, at times, actually done away with it. Closer examination shows, however, that while elimination of this rift has often been announced, many hurdles make reconciliation between the life forces of religion and sex exceedingly difficult to reach. The rift between these two forces, therefore, remains quite latent everywhere—in theology, the Church, Christianity and all of society. Several examples of this could be recently observed, both in Europe and in the United States.

Let us remember, first of all, the revolt of priests against the downgrading of sexuality and women which theology and Church achieved through celibacy. Reliable research among clergy[4] and laity shows that the majority of Catholics oppose celibacy and wish to eliminate the rift between sex and religion. The German news magazine *Der Spiegel* reported in January 1967 that a survey conducted by the Emnid Institute in Bielefeld[5] showed that 84 per cent of the German population favor marriage of a priest. This survey provided separate results from Catholic and non-Catholic groups: 95 per cent of Protestants, and 96 per cent of those who did not identify themselves with any religious denomination, favored priestly marriage; more than two-thirds, or 69 per cent, of German Catholics shared this view. The younger the Catholic population, the more it favored priestly marriage. Among those 60–70 years old, only 59 per cent held this view; but the percentage among 50–59-year-old persons rose to 69 per cent. Among those from 35–49 years, it rose to 70 per cent; with those aged 25–34 it rose to 73 per cent; and with those aged 18–24 it reached 77 per cent.

The survey showed that, regardless of age, sex or social background, a clear majority favored lifting the celibacy rule. The report said, "Even among Catholics who are regular churchgoers, more than half, or 58 per cent, believe that priests should be permitted to marry."[6] In 1970, press reports showed that among Dutch bishops only 5 per cent wanted to retain the current link between priesthood and celibacy. In 1969, 72 per cent of Catholics in Holland decided against celibacy.[7]

In spite of rejection of celibacy, a negative latent Dualism can be observed behind the many positive attitudes toward priestly marriage. As an example, I would like to cite the well-known theologian Hans Küng, who is certainly neither conservative nor traditionalist. But just because he is regarded as progressive and liberal, it is instructive to study a passage from his book *Wahrhaftigkeit*.[8] He writes as follows: "If the Catholic priest Davis[9] had married without simultaneously leaving the Church, his action could at least have been regarded as an indirect clear-cut open protest: a protest against the law (*not the charisma!*) of non-marriage for priests."[10] But if non-marriage for priests is regarded as a charisma contrary to marriage, then we are dealing with a consistent perpetuation of the rift between sexuality and religion. The Greek word *charisma* means "gift of grace," whereas in the New Testament charisma stands for a mysterious inner power which acts within man as *charis*—"divine grace," such as in the gift of clairvoyance, speaking in tongues[11] or the gift of healing.[12] If non-marriage for priests is considered charisma, then God regards as his élite force only men who are weak in their sex drives, impotent and hostile toward sex and women. According to this view, he favors those who, to put it positively, have a special "gift of sexlessness," or, to put it negatively, those who are impotent. This, however, is debasing to all men who wish to live as God made them—as human beings with sexual needs whose satisfaction provides pleasure, serenity, harmony among men generally and among the sexes in particular. A theology that aims at healing the rift between sex and religion would use the label "charisma" only for people who are particularly gifted with a sex drive and sexual potency, well equipped to make a sexual partner happy.

Yet another example for a latent discrepancy between sexuality and religion was the reaction in the United States to a book by William E. Phipps, entitled *Was Jesus Married?*[13] The guess that Jesus was married is not new[14] and to the believing Christian rather irrelevant; whether Christ was married or not, and assuming that the value of sexuality has not really been internalized, there is no particular relationship between man's sex life and his belief in the life as Christ. That, however, is exactly the case in the so-called Christian world. The result was as follows: When Phipps first expressed his intention of writing a book on the marriage of Christ, which he did in an article, he received many letters from angry Christians who regarded the assumption that Christ had a sex life as a greater sacrilege than the idea that "God is dead."[15] Most Christians agree with Emil Brunner who said, "We cannot imagine that Our Lord was married."[16]

A good empirical verification of my thesis that the rift between sexuality and religion remains latent between theology and society can be found in a book by Friedrich Koch dealing with negative and positive sexual education.[17] Koch analyzes the German literature on sexual education as provided in Catholic, Protestant and ecumenical works.[18] He states that the material surveyed contains only few segments that show evidence of obvious downgrading of the body. He speaks of a "latent Manichaeanism" in present-day society. He agrees with Hans Müller-Eckhard who believes, on the basis of psychiatric treatment of sexual neurotics, that "Christian civilization has contradicted Manichaeanism, but has merely forced it into a state of latency, where it continues to simmer quietly and secretly."[19]

Koch feels that his research indicates "expressions of a greater or lesser latent Manichaeanism, a general feeling that dignity is to be found in the area of the spiritual and mental, whereas the body is treated with skepticism and contempt."[20] The role of the body becomes still clearer in the description of feelings encountered in writings on sexual education. Bodily experiences are transformed into dimensions of the soul, and sexual pleasure is only seen as the basis of soul experiences. Thus, it is regarded as morally wrong and sinful "when married couples degrade the love encounter into a pleasurable act, because the love experience is thereby distorted into a lust experience."[21]

We are now able to ascertain whether the rift between sex and religion may be bridged: Yes, this *theoretically* is quite possible. Factors do exist—criticism of the Encyclical *Humanae Vitae;* increasing elimination of the contrast between matter and spirit; desexualization of asceticism; the priest revolt against celibacy—all these give the impression that this rift will not last much longer. Certain Protestant and Catholic viewpoints even give the impression that theology and the Church have become more cordial toward sex. However, elimination of the rift between sex and religion continues to encounter strong resistance in practical application. Current viewpoints seek to show that, after centuries of a marriage morality antagonistic to sex, sexual intercourse in marriage may under specific circumstances actually be good. They do not evaluate sexuality as such but only sexual relations in marriage. But sexuality is an independent life force; it

exists without reference to theological and churchly laws
or sanctions that continue to oppose and to satanize it.

The continued latent rift between sex and religion
erupts into open conflict whenever Churches are forced
to comment officially on sexual matters or involve themselves in matters of government unrelated to the immediate duties of the clergy. Here are two examples: the Holy
See's ruling that in the future all Catholic priests are to
use Holy Thursday to renew annually their pledges of
chastity and obedience;[22] Protestant-Catholic opposition
to reforms in marital and civil law, which the Social Democratic Party intends to undertake in Germany.[23] Behind
these and other events stands the attitude of theologians
and churchmen that the Church is a guardian who must
see to it that sex, being a dangerous antagonist of religion, is suppressed as often and successfully as possible.

V SEXUALITY BETWEEN RELIGION AND SOCIETY

21. Results of Christian Antagonism to Sex

I

Our major finding, that the separation between religion and sex is nearly insurmountable, should be sufficient to show that Christian antagonism to sex has irrevocably damaged the two great life forces, religion and sexuality, thereby severely injuring humanity, society, the Churches and all of Christendom. The enemies of all that is good and true have reaped vast benefits from this animosity, which has hastened the dehumanization of man. Yet, further disastrous results emerge from Christianity's warfare against sex, by its impact on secular society and bourgeois "morality." The genitocentric nature of this morality contributed disastrously to the history of so-called Christian nations, which has encompassed such horrible examples as the Auschwitz extermination camp and the My Lai massacre during the Vietnam war. This "morality," which claims to be valid for all mankind, has greatly reduced Christianity's ability to serve the humanization of man.

Hidden behind the screen of a "divine" and "moral" society are those frustrated bourgeois types who carefully conceal their own character from the scrutiny of their fellow men. The pursuit of success on a social and career level calls for lip service to a morality that simply eludes enforcement because it runs counter to nature and is antagonistic to human nature. Under these conditions, lies and hypocrisy become virtues. The ethics of success, designed for gain in everyday life, advance at the price of ethical responsibility. The ideal road to success in life implies that the individual say A, mean B, and do C. As bourgeois "morality" is basically antagonistic to sex, the success ethic means that whoever represses his sexual needs most skillfully, or satisfies them secretly, enhances his chances for a career that has middle-class approval. Repression of sex and sexual needs is linked with the repression of independent thought and action. As a result, bourgeois society has replaced freedom, love and joy—which correspond to the teachings of Christ—with hatred, suffering and the individual's dependence on various "morality" pressures against all who might wish to say A, mean A and act A.

The genitocentric morality of bourgeois society, with its antagonism toward sex, has removed itself so far from its "Christian" origins that one might question whether Christianity bears quite as much guilt in its development as is generally assumed. The Belgian historian J. van Ussel even advances the thesis that "the bourgeoization of society has resulted in a completely new type of man, as well as in new interpersonal relations, socio-economic conditions and therefore in a new anti-sexual attitude."[1] According to this view, emancipation of sex is only possible if man has been freed from his bourgeois impact. That is totally untrue! The bourgeois development of society toward a new antisexual position could only take place on the basis of theological and churchly views which were supposed to reflect "God's will" and had a Christian meta-

physical foundation. Bourgeois morality and institutionalized Christianity are closely linked. This is clearly shown
whenever sexual emancipation is halted by resistance
from the Churches, or when bourgeois society supports
the persecution of sexually emancipated men and women
with arguments of theological or churchly origin, such as
claiming that "the meaning and result of sexual intercourse is the child."

II

The unholy alliance between institutionalized Christianity and bourgeois society, designed to control man
through antisexual laws, is among the most regrettable
results of Christian sexual morality. We owe to this alliance the commercialization of sex and such side effects
as crimes that can take place only in a society that im-
prisons its members within a certain "morality." This society can function only when the lie, hypocrisy and similar
elements have replaced candor and natural, spontaneous
experiences. This alliance is responsible for modern man's
inability to free himself from bourgeois "morality." Sexual
inability in the vital areas of life manifests itself daily; at
least the so-called Christian part of the world proves Sigmund Freud's observation that all of mankind is his
patient.[2]

Inability to free oneself from bourgeois "morality" can
be found in daily life where physicians and educators are
unable to help those struggling with sexual problems. A
member of the Hamburg Institute for Sexual Research,
Volkmar Sigusch, reported to the sixth German Clinical
Convention in 1970[3] that doctors are not educationally
equipped to help their patients' sexual difficulties. They
tend to ignore sexual problems consciously, often using

cures that reflect a physician's militant attitude against
sex. Medical research has failed to explore the area of
sexuality without prejudice, and medical men tend to view
it within the "rigid patterns of society." Sigusch believes
that physicians have permitted themselves to act as "servants of official sexual ideology."[4]

In far too many countries, Germany being only one of
them, medical textbooks concentrate on an outdated ideology that sees sex exclusively in the service of procreation; the concept of sexuality for its own self, purely as a
source of enjoyment, is viewed by medical men as suspect
and labeled as pathological. Two East German professors,
Franz and Margarete Fleck, classify not only masturbation
and homosexuality as "sexual abnormalities and confu-
sions" but also regard as pathological "petting and extramarital relations."[5] This example, drawn from the German
Democratic Republic (GDR), proves that the power of
bourgeois "morality" and of its antisexual Dualism retains
control even in societies opposed to bourgeois mentality.
We should not ignore that the GDR regards bourgeois
sexual morality as a welcome and reliable instrument in
the rule of the East German regime.

Educators also fail to aid the young generation in the
sexual area. This emerges from the interesting research
undertaken by Klaus Thomas,[6] a psychologist, medical
man and theologian. Thomas has decades of experience
among people who are at odds with life and whose sui-
cidal tendencies are in need of control. He has found that
most of those considering suicide had no, or only an im-
perfect, sexual education; this gap led to conflicts, failures, neuroses and difficulties in everyday life.[7] This is not
only true of Germany, but even in countries of stronger
democratic traditions. Similar failures in sex education
are cited[8] by Alexander Sutherland Neill: "I have never

had a pupil who did not bring to Summerhill a diseased attitude toward sexuality and bodily functions. The children of modern parents who were told the truth about where babies come from have much the same hidden attitude toward sex that the children of religious fanatics have. To find a new orientation to sex is the most difficult task of the parent and teacher."[9]

III

Klaus Thomas' handbook of suicide prevention[10] provides considerable insight into the results of man's inability to free himself from antisexual morality. Thomas shows that the religious life creates maximum mental sufferings among clergymen who are trapped between views they must advance officially and the actual demands of everyday reality. Thomas shows in his chapter on Protestant churchmen[11] that 12 per cent of those considering suicide who consulted the author were clergy, wives of clergy, teachers of religion or students at religious seminaries. Thomas rightly regards this as the largest self-contained professional group among the desperate and potential suicides.[12] Thomas' findings create the unmistakable picture of an *ecclesiogene neurosis;* that is, a neurosis founded on the influence of the Church. Parallel difficulties among Catholic priests have not as yet been carefully studied, but the celibacy controversy and the revolt of the priests suggest that it is at least as great as among their Protestant colleagues.

The inability of Catholicism to free itself from its sexual morality was well summarized by the German news magazine *Der Spiegel* in 1970. It stated: "All over the world an Unholy War is in progress. It is a war with victims who are not dead and with missing persons for whom no one

is searching. It is a war that has already been lost by the
man who started it: Pope Paul VI. He is trying to defend
the celibacy he calls divine, while destroying the remaining authority of papal rule."[13] The defense of celibacy,
which in today's society embodies what theologians and
Churches have advanced for centuries, not only boom-
erangs against papal rule but against the Church and all
of Christianity as well.

Among the negative results of this policy is a withdrawal
of youth from the ministry and the resulting high age
bracket among Catholic priests. By now, every fourth
clergyman in France is over sixty years old. A study by
the French Institute for Demographic Research shows that
some 27 per cent of male clergy are more than sixty years
old. By comparison, the national average of this age group
is about 21 per cent. Among female members of religious
orders, the danger of too high an age group is even more
striking. Among them, those over sixty amounted to 41.5
per cent. Among male clergy, some 48 per cent are between the ages of forty and fifty-nine. Whereas in the
generally active and employed population those under
forty total 57.73 per cent, the ratio among priests is only
24.22 per cent.[14] The Institute's report states: "The rules
concerning chastity tend to prompt young Catholics to
avoid priestly offices, although there is general concern
about a shortage of clergy."[15]

Finally, we find in our society, both profane and sacred,
a total debasement of the word "love." This, too, is an
outgrowth of bourgeois "morality." The word "love" is
now used as a synonym for the sex act ("making love");
alternatively, the concept of love is totally removed from
the area of the sexual, particularly where bourgeois "morality" is guided by Christian concepts that marriage without love is better than love without marriage. The

exclusion of love from relations between the sexes emerges from one of the documents published after the Second Vatican Council, the *Motuproprio*, concerning legal order of mixed marriages.[16] At first it appeared that my criticism of *Motuproprio* might have been premature, based as it was on an early translation from the Latin; but when I examined a translation furnished by German bishops, I had to agree with Heinz Josef Herbort who concluded, with startling accuracy, "Pope Paul VI, in his most recent *Motuproprio*, refers 40 times to marriage among members of different denominations. He speaks of Law, Righteousness, Norm, Duty and Obedience, but never once of Love."[17]

22. Between Religion and Government

Societies that set themselves up as defenders of the Christian Occident and its values, actually have little use for such genuine Christian concepts as love, freedom, social justice or peace. The same is true of societies that advocate a bourgeois morality based on "Christian concepts" and exploit the word "Christian" to enhance their positions.

The history of Christian nations teaches us that such nations are often particularly warlike. When it comes to the exploitation of weaker countries, in colonialism or slave trade, their "Christian" conscience is easily silenced. The sexual life of their population is often governed by their rulers, who profess agreement with "Men of God" that suppression of sexuality is "God's will" and that man's sexual emancipation contradicts the teachings of Christ. We can trace a correlation between the severe demands such societies or rulers make on the population and the genitocentric morality reflected by its ethical forms. The greater the demand made by rulers on their fellow men, the stricter their controls over the private, sexual lives of the ruled.

The writings of Wilhelm Reich, as well as more recent publications, show that the strictest sacral and profane individuals, institutions and systems put a high value on morality; they know that sexually repressed people are relatively easy to manipulate. The repressed are more easily used and abused, particularly for causes that would repel a true Christian. Sexually repressed people are not only easy to manipulate but quite ready to participate in crimes that satisfy sadomasochistic needs caused by sexual frustration.

It is easy to agree with Erich Fromm[1] that authoritarian society structures create and satisfy precisely the needs that grow from sadomasochism. The satisfaction of sadomasochistic needs is both negative and positive. Fromm writes correctly: "It is negative, as a liberation from anxiety, because it provides security by dependence on a powerful force; it is positive in satisfying individual desires for influence and strength by submission to this power."[2] In such situations, independent thought and action are impossible, and the rule of men over men is doubly assured. The number of those ready to help their criminal rulers increases while all who might undermine the rule of men over men face destruction. Quite often they are destroyed in the name of "Christian morality."

II

Among the numerous examples that illustrate relations between religion, sexuality and governmental rule, I wish to cite Tommaso Campanella's[3] book *Città del Sole* (*The Sun State*).[4] I quote from this fictional, "utopian" work[5] —although it dates back more than three centuries—to show the ultimate goals of a universal papal monarchy, the image of a state governed by supermen in clerical

positions. Campanella's book imagines a utopian state, totally Christian-Communistic, governed by an ideal Pope[6]
and by priests who exercise unhampered control over human souls. This "Sun State," totally enclosed by walls, was
described by the strongly Church-oriented Dominican
Campanella in all detail.

The state he envisioned is governed by a priestly prince,
named "Metaphysicus," who unites all spiritual and
worldly powers in his hand. He is aided by three princes
named "Power, Wisdom and Love." Power looks after affairs of war; Wisdom deals with economics, the arts and
education; while Love is in charge of public welfare.
Metaphysicus always acts in agreement with his three supporting princes, but nothing takes place without his own
approval, and all matters of state are undertaken jointly
by all four. Whatever seems good to Metaphysicus has
the total agreement of everyone else.

The inhabitants of this Sun State are completely controlled through the confessions which all government
agencies require for their constant rule over the souls of
the populace. All citizens confess their sins in secrecy to
those above them, "who at the same time purify these
souls and discover what errors occur most frequently
among the inhabitants. Higher officials, in turn, confess
their sins to the three highest leaders, advise them simultaneously of the missteps of others, although without naming them and only in general terms, even concerning the
most serious and state-endangering actions. The three
princes, in turn, confess these sins as well as their own
to Metaphysicus, who thus knows precisely whatever un-
lawful acts might be going on in his State and who can
take the necessary countermeasures. He offers a sacrifice
to God and prays; but first he confesses to God the sins of
the whole nation, publicly, from the altar of the Temple.

This is done whenever forgiveness is required, but again without naming any sinner by name. He thus frees the nation of its sins, urging it to be on guard against forbidden actions; he then makes a sacrifice to God, asking him to forgive the citizens, deliver them of their sins, enlighten and guard them. Once a year, the highest princes of each subordinate state publicly confess the sins of their inhabitants to Metaphysicus. He is thus aware of any negative developments in the provinces and is able to advise everyone on worldly and spiritual levels."[7]

When one knows that everyone—particularly the upper echelon of officialdom—within the Sun State is a priest whose task is to cleanse the public's consciousness, we have the perfect picture of a priestly dictatorship that rules out all opinions differing from those of the ideal Pope and clergy. The views and convictions of sexual life among inhabitants of the Sun State agree with those the Catholic Church seeks to impose on its followers. Campanella, or the rulers of the Sun State he outlined, would like to enforce a morality that views sexual intercourse exclusively for purposes of procreation and labels everything that varies from this norm as sinful. Campanella gave high priority to absolute Church rule extending into the bedrooms of society and eliminating all independent thought and action. Total rule is assured because the citizen is observed and controlled in his most intimate sphere, in every detail that goes into the creation of that sphere.

We read, for instance, that citizens of the Sun State must observe the following rules:

"No woman may be linked to a man until she has reached the nineteenth year. No man may impregnate before he has reached the twenty-first year. . . . Prior to this, only a few women are permitted to meet with men, only those who are sterile or pregnant, so that they may not be forced to seek unnatural outlets. Old women and officials provide love enjoyment to those who are too passionate or experience too strong a drive, depending on how they have been secretly observed in the sports arena. Permission for this activity is given by the highest officials concerned with procreational activities, the chief physician who belongs to the Ministry of 'Love.'

"Whoever is found to practice sodomy is called to order and must, as a punishment, have his shoes tied around his neck for two days, showing that he had turned the order of things upside down, so that his foot is where his head should be. If he commits the same act again, punishment is made more severe and finally the death sentence is imposed. Those, however, who refrain from intercourse up to the age of twenty-one, and particularly those who refrain from it up to the age of twenty-seven, are celebrated at special meetings with speeches and songs.[8]

"After the manner of the ancient Spartans, men and women engage in sports totally nude. In this way, supervising officials know which men and women are ready for conception and which men and women are bodily most suited for each other. Only then, and after taking a bath, do they make themselves ready for their love activity. Tall and beautiful women are linked with tall and active men, fat women are mated with thin men, and slender women with heavy-set men, so that things will even themselves out. Children come in the evening and prepare the bedroom. Then, the man and woman go to bed, under the *supervision of appropriate male and female officials*. But they do not begin sexual union before they have digested their food and offered a prayer to God. The women have the opportunity of observing portraits of famous men in their bedrooms. They are also able to look through their windows up to heaven and to ask God to bless them with strong children. Until the hour of union, men and women sleep in two separate chambers. Then one of the *female supervisors* opens both doors from the outside. The appropriate hour is *fixed* by astrologers and physicians."[9]

III

Campanella's ideal state, reminiscent of George Orwell's[10] pessimistic Utopia, *1984,* has never been realized within the framework of Catholicism. One may say, however, that the Catholic Church has constantly attempted to prepare the groundwork for such absolute clerical rule over the private lives of the faithful. Confession has been the most important medium of social control, forming one of the most important bases for the practices Campanella envisioned. Following the rules layed down by the Lateran Council of 1215, every believer must make his annual confession before a priest, enabling the Church to study and manipulate the conscience of Catholics.

Because confession provides continual monitoring of the rule of men by men, it concentrates on the sexual area of anyone offering confession. Men who go to confession come to hate women, their own bodies and all sexually related matters. We see, for instance, the following in a leaflet on Hell,[11] concerning confession: "Observe the body you occupy! How does it manage below? Your eyes that have sinned, that have viewed with lust, have concentrated too much on worldly beauty and vanity, they are as flames, see no ray of light and know merely

an outer and internal darkness. Regardless of the darkness
of Hell, they can observe the horror of condemned creatures, the anger of the torturing devils, the pleasures with
which they enjoy your suffering. Your ears, while on earth,
listened to sinful talk with pleasure or have otherwise
sinned, and now they are aflame! Have you had an ear-
ache? They can be terrible. But what are they in comparison to the sufferings of your ears in Hell? . . . Look
upon your hands which have probably sinned much, committed horrible sins. They have violated and thus they
must suffer. . . . Your whole body, its flesh filled with sin,
will boil as in a fire! With what greed the flames lick this
body!"[12]

Where the Church is no longer able to rule by means of
sexual suppression, it allies itself with worldly powers that
exist by fighting the liberation of humanity which Christ
desired. A classic example of such an unholy alliance was
the Concordat between Fascist Italy and the Vatican[13]
of 1929, which enabled the Church to rule even over men
who did not belong to it. To this day, neo-Fascists and
Catholics in Italy try jointly to safeguard their former
co-operation at the price of liberty and democracy. They
seek to prevent the democratic Republic of Italy from
realizing what Christ sought: to free men from the rule
of men over men. Just how unholy the alliance between
fascism and Catholicism can be is shown by their joint
negative position on divorce. While the Vatican and its
Italian allies speak of marriage as an insoluble bond, the
actual condition of marriage in Italy has deteriorated into
a national disgrace. "Every year only about ten thousand
marriages are legally dissolved. Those who achieve legal
divorce may not marry again. Legally, their marriage continues and hypocrisy is officially condoned."[14]

23. Sex and Freedom

When we speak of freedom, we usually ignore the truism that no one who is either ruler or ruled can actually be free.[1] Most people only care that they themselves are not ruled but are quite ready to dominate others. For this reason, a good deal of the talk about freedom quickly deteriorates into an empty ritual; much that is said on this subject simply lacks conviction.[2] Quite often, those who speak of freedom think of their fellow men as lacking in liberty only because their thoughts and actions are different from their own.

We can easily find the seeds of intolerance, hidden under the kind of freedom that would get rid of all freedoms. Often those who wrap themselves in the mantle of freedom only seek to force their own ideology and life style on others. They advocate their own convictions as the only road to salvation and do not hesitate to use many techniques of force to bring others under their dominance. These others are only guilty of thinking that no one may have a monopoly on freedom, that no one is qualified to decide who *is* free or who *shall* be free.

We must keep these dangers constantly in mind and

remain aware of the role that different value concepts play in our society. We depend on the exercise of a pluralism of values, on the conscious and free endorsements of safeguards against all demands for a single value system, endorsed by those who seek to decide on the freedom and order of their community. Pluralism of values is essential to any society that offers its members the guarantee that they may act and think as free human beings. Wherever the supply and demand on the market of values is ample, the individual's need for an independent decision becomes correspondingly great. This can enable an ideal type to unfold, true to the concept "Do not rule; do not be ruled." Religion may either serve as a restraining or encouraging force of the type of freedom as we understand it here.

As in the case of freedom generally, sexual freedom is in danger of being subjected to faulty guidelines. Societies that fully accept masturbation, sexual play among the young, premarital coitus, homosexuality and all coitus positions as well as non-coital experiences are sexually liberated. Where the possibilities of choice are restricted, are differently valued or fixed, freedom is restricted.[3] Limited sexual freedom is often permitted only to enable the rule of men over men to function more effectively in other areas of life. Into this category falls the tolerance and social acceptance of prostitution by societies that place a high value on virginity. Masculine society can enforce its dominance over "respectable" women only when it disposes of an army of "valueless females" whose main function is the satisfaction of masculine sexual needs. The "respectable" woman can thus remain man's property, protected, isolated and subject to his total rule.

We find, therefore, that sexual freedom does not necessarily imply a favorable attitude toward sex and women.

Conversely, certain restrictions of sexual freedom need not indicate a hatred of women or hostility toward sex. Such limitations may be motivated by magical-religious anxieties, above all by fear of the opposite sex. These fears tend to contribute to taboos and to laws that control man's sexual activity. Sexual liberty and a positive attitude toward women and sex exist only where sexual freedom is accompanied by proof that sexuality in all its functions —including the function of play—is specifically endorsed as a source of joy.

II

The so-called Christian West was never able to combine sexual freedom with a positive attitude toward women and sex. To begin with, the antisexual Dualism of institutionalized Christianity sought to force man's sexual habits into the mold of a marriage morality which limited sexual freedom to a minimum. Further, various rulers learned early to use Christian morality for purposes of sexual suppression in order to gain maximum leverage for their dominance over other men. Wherever absolutism gained control, woman was downgraded and sexual freedom restricted. Rulers tended to fit sexual freedom into their own patterns, even when it seemed that they were advocating sexual freedom. National socialism in Germany, a profane masculine movement, lived up to these theses as well as others, such as that woman haters are also freedom haters, or that anxiety about sex leads to fear of freedom.

The Nazi view of women, of woman's social role, has recently been examined by Wolfgang Philipp[4] by comparing Nordic (Indo-Germanic) and Western (Island-Celtic) women. We also gain insight from the work of

Theodor Friedrich[5] who opposed the women's movement
as endangering "motherhood" to a point where "woman
had become the enemy of woman."[6] The Nazi concept of
woman, actually a form of hate, was summarized by Fritz
von Unruh, who wrote, "A minimum of intellect and a
maximum of physical usefulness makes woman what she
should be: The Womb of the Third Reich."[7] The National
Socialists agreed with their Führer that the meaning and
aim of marriage was "the increase of tribe and race."[8]

The morality of the Nazis, who alleged that they
wanted to halt the decline of the Christian West, was
shown in a talk by Gestapo Chief Heinrich Himmler, who
liked to pose as a "Concerned" Superfather. He told leaders of the Nazi Élite Corps (SS) in Poznan (October 4,
1944) that their morality should be as follows: "The SS
man must follow one basic concept: We have to remain
honest, responsible, loyal and comradely only toward
those who share our blood, but to no one else. What happens to the Russians or what happens to the Czechs does
not concern me. Whatever good is within these people,
in terms of blood, that we shall obtain—if need be, by
robbing them of their children and bringing them up.
Whether these other people live well, or starve to death,
interests me only in order to decide whether we can use
them as slaves of our own civilization; nothing else concerns me. When we build a fortification and ten-thousand
Russian women collapse from fatigue, that interests me
only if it endangers the completion of these fortresses
for Germany. Wherever possible, we shall refrain from
being needlessly ruthless and heartless; that much is clear.
We Germans, who are alone in the world in having a decent attitude toward animals, shall retain a decent attitude
toward these human animals as well; but it would be a
crime against our own blood to worry about them and

to meet them with ideals that could hamper the task of our sons and grandsons."[9]

It seems no accident that such a "morality" should have developed in the so-called Christian West. The National Socialists were a profane masculine movement that encountered a readymade "culture" in the masculine society of the Churches. These genuine Christian values of love and freedom had been abandoned in favor of one-sided genitocentric morality. The Nazis' use of women to enhance the race invites comparisons with the Churches, to the detriment of institutional Christianity. We have only to remember its Satanization of women[10] in order to realize that the Nazi concept of women, hatred of women, has a very long prehistory in the Christian West.

III

Institutionalized Christianity denied sexual freedom not only because of antagonism to sex, but because of its uneasy relation to freedom generally. The Reformation enabled Christians to rediscover the truth that man has an inherent right to freedom. True, the Churches continued to hold on to their social past. Yet, the post-Reformation years provided society with dynamic new impulses that permitted and encouraged numerous egalitarian movements directed against social inequality and the dominance of men over men. This hastened the process of man's emotional maturity. It helped in liberating man, permitting a fresh link-up with a revolutionary biblical spirit, quite independent of the Churches trapped in their own social past. Such historical phenomena as the Enlightenment, the French Revolution or socialism may be seen as the functional equivalents of Christian beliefs. Such beliefs, even when not technically Christian, contain

significant sociological aspects corresponding to Christian
viewpoints. These express a Christian spirit which often
contradicts the attitude that institutionalized Christianity
displays toward freedom, equality and justice. These convictions represent a type of humanism which today seeks
to advance through many different struggles and sac-
rifices.

This thesis can be documented in many ways. I wish
to use it, together with other arguments, to counter such
assertions as the view that contemporary society has been
de-Christianized.[11] I wish to cite, to counter such views,
the position of woman in relation to sexual freedom. Concerning socialism in particular, August Bebel has spoken
of the women's movement within socialism, and of all
other suppressed groups, in his book on women and socialism.[12] He stated that "the Social Democratic party
is the *only* party that has spoken up in favor of equality
for woman, her liberation from all dependency and suppression, not for reasons of party propaganda but as a
necessity."[13] Bebel felt that there can be no human liberation without the social independence and equality of
sexes,[14] and he thus served the ideas of Christ better than
many woman haters who call themselves Christians.

It is difficult to deny that socialism is the only movement that wishes to achieve woman's independence from
man and therefore speaks up for sexual freedom. This
excludes the error of a bourgeois pseudo-sexual liberation
which amounts to brutalization of the sexual and uses
women as a commodity to be traded and degraded. Militant Catholicism holds socialism responsible for the alleged sexual revolution of the present day.[15] It thus makes
clear that institutionalized Christianity continues to fear
freedom and therefore insists on opposing all movements
that advocate man's personal freedom which, in turn, is

allied to sexual freedom. The Churches refuse to realize that, as Radhakrishnan put it, "when we submit too much to the laws of the past, when the living faith of the dead becomes the dead faith of the living, our civilization will disappear. We must undertake reasonable changes. Whenever an organism loses the power to eliminate its excrements, it dies. Freedom belongs to the living; the spirit of freedom does not reject the past, but fulfills its promises."[16]

24. Man Comes of Age

Institutionalized Christianity offers many examples which show that a religion, a philosophy, an institution, a society or a state can offer sexual freedom only when it has a positive attitude toward sex and women. Freedom can only be respected as a whole. Where socialism exists in an institutionalized form, as "socialism from above," it adopts the same institutionalized pattern as Christianity, and is capable of the distortion or total elimination of freedom. The moment socialism ignores its own primary concepts, respect for the individual and the struggle for free human development,[1] it degenerates into another form of rule by men over men.[2]

Wherever socialism forces the individual to surrender himself to the collectivism of a party or class, we encounter phenomena that remind us of the Church of the Middle Ages. It is significant to our theme that wherever socialism means rule of men over men, its morality comes to resemble that of the *bourgeoisie*. The less socialism respects man's right to freedom, the more it will control the what, how, where or when of a satisfaction of sexual needs. It is, therefore, no accident that the Soviet Union frowns upon extramarital relations, regards public display of affection among young people as inappropriate, and employs special youth raiders (*Drushinniky*) in its parks of culture to enforce respectability after dark.[3]

The journalist Ada Baskina reported in the Moscow *Literary Gazette*[4] that sexology and sexual pathology are quite underdeveloped in the puritanic USSR, that Russians are surprisingly ignorant of physiological differences between men and women. She reports that until 1969 no book on sexual education had been published in the Soviet Union and that the first marital guide, translated from a book published in East Germany, was not available for open sale in bookstores but restricted to libraries. Of course, this resulted in long waiting lists in the libraries. Mrs. Baskina acted as a marriage counselor but provided no sexual education, limiting herself instead to household advice.[5]

This tendency is reminiscent of the traditional role of woman in German bourgeois society, where she was limited to children, kitchen and church. Of course, the party or state in East Germany has replaced the Church. Just how much in agreement bourgeois and Socialist morality may become, wherever they seek to rule men by morality, is illustrated by the views of a conservative Swiss marital consultant, Theodor Bovet, who praised the tyranny of Joseph Stalin because he used the 1930s "to turn the steering wheel around and introduced a new discipline into the institution of marriage. It was one of the most important deeds and expressions of his realistic concepts."[6]

II

How do we explain the development of a morality that deprives man of his freedom and puts him into a controlled position? This question applies particularly to so-

cieties that go under the name of Christianity or socialism
and that state that they are devoted to the liberation of
man from all oppression. But neither Christianity nor socialism, in their institutionalized forms, truly serve man;
instead, they favor those who utter promising slogans concerning justice, brotherhood and freedom to gain power
over their fellow men. But a free-thinking man forever
questions the powerful, and they therefore wish to limit
the number of those who have truly come of age. Still, a
system that calls itself Christian should never ignore or
disdain the basic truth that a society oriented to Christ's
teaching must be made up of men who are free to think,
decide and act independently. We can judge from the
number of men who are truly mature, to what degree a
society considers its Christianity essential.

Christian faith, particularly the belief in Christ and his
teaching, enables man to think and act independently.
As long as institutionalized Christianity takes such faith
seriously, it encourages man's independence from all
worldly power, enabling him to free himself from evil,
independent of any group that demands political, social
or financial commitment. A Christianity that takes Christ's
teachings seriously permits the individual freely to find
salvation within the framework offered by Christ. Christianity is a religion of individuals. Their success or failure
depends on whether the successors of Christ, who admin-
ister Christianity in his name, educate Christians to formulate thought and action on the basis of a free and personal
decision for Christ, while bearing a personal responsibility
for such thought and action.

Increasing collectivization and institutionalization of
Christianity offered the Churches the irresistible temptation, while acting as legitimate successors of Christ, to
strengthen their power at the price of Christian freedom.

They demanded not freedom but total dependence of the individual on the Church and on its "divine demands" that sanctioned laws which were to influence the individual's inner struggle. Yet, evil, not salvation, was the result. Christians conscious of their responsibility have acted in favor of individual freedom, responding to the separation of the Church from Christ's teaching and the resulting disasters. By means of personal faith and charisma, these men achieved reformation of the individual in the West. Personal religious legitimacy enabled man to seek salvation through independent thought and action.

True, Martin Luther was subject in his own thought and theology to the vertical structure of a society within which he lived and worked. It can also not be denied that John Calvin and his theocratic system vacillated between aristocracy and a distorted form of oligarchy. Yet, because Luther and the Reformation enabled men to rediscover their integral right to freedom, he helped them decisively to achieve individual liberation and thus to mature; to come of age. Calvinism eventually helped to turn Christianity toward democratic thought and provided bases for a society that permitted the individual to resist the rule of men over men. Calvin rejected state rule over man's conscience and provided the Calvinist of Scotland, England and Holland with theological bases for the freedom struggle that became particularly significant in these regions. John Knox (Scotland) as well as the Presbyterians and Puritans (England) gained from the democratic concept of the state a metaphysical legitimacy and dynamic that helped the concept of freedom to unprecedented success.

The moment the individual made personal faith the single criterion of value, he realized that salvation could only be achieved when he acted in accordance with his own faith. This created a constructive pluralism as well as the struggle for a society that could assure individual freedom and thus a road to salvation based on individual conviction. This enables us to understand certain egalitarian movements, struggles against social inequality and against every form of rule by men over men. It is instructive to view these within the framework of a value system that began with the discovery that the individual possesses an inborn aspiration to freedom, once he seeks to create his individuality, while achieving respect for others. We can find a formulation for this rediscovery of truth—in the spirit of Christ, which is freedom—in the eighteenth paragraph of the Universal Declaration of Human Rights (December 10, 1948) which said: "Every man has the right to demand freedom of thought, conscience and religion."

Institutionalized Christianity continues to depend on the power of its laws and on its allies in state and society who enforce these laws with its judges and police forces. But Christ-Come-of-Age sees to it that the work of Christ in the service of man's total liberation moves toward completion. More precisely: Christ-Come-of-Age struggles for the realization of the eighteenth paragraph of the Universal Declaration of Human Rights because such realization opens new possibilities to the humanization of man. With this goes a new morality that would oust various institutions, notably the Church, from the bedroom of mature man.

Few men can truly be described as having come of age. This is one reason why theologians and the Church continue to be able to use the name of Christianity to guide man's sexual life in detail, aided by the state and its representatives. Among the many fashionable slogans of theology—that have little relation to life's reality—belongs the observation that Christians of the post-Reformation period were already mature. Man-Come-of-Age is not a reality but a possibility that resulted from the Reformation. Fear of possible total freedom is still stronger than the power of freedom. We have seen emergence from one tyranny, followed by surrender to the success ethic, denial of responsibility, abandonment of truth—all in support of the allegation that only he is truly of age who knows the limits of his freedom. There continues to exist a strong effort on the part of rulers within profane and sacred systems to hold down the number of men who might be truly called being of age. We can't say truthfully that man, even after Luther, has actually come of age. The existence of those who have come of age continues to be hampered by the number of those still unfree, who consciously or unconsciously enable men to rule over other men.

This does not mean that the existence of those who are truly mature is narrower or more difficult than before. On the contrary, the few who have achieved maturity contribute to the doubts that now surround authoritarian persons or institutions which act *ex cathedra*. They have also aided the younger generation in accepting only the authority of those who have won, by means of personal charisma, close relations with their fellow men. Mature man creates a healthy kind of unrest. He encourages the world's desire, wherever authority can only succeed when it is convincing, that what it demands and says is actually the truth. The chances of mature man increase whenever he brings his environment to accept a relationship between order and freedom, replacing a rule of man over man and thus developing a more humane pattern than was offered by the early patriarchal structure of society.

Concretely speaking, mature man has to prove that his sexual emancipation has nothing whatever to do with the fashionable sexual pseudo freedom that manifests itself in today's so-called sexual revolution; it does not appeal to the truly free, but only to the totally submissive man. It is not the mature man who brings about this "revolution," but the type who overthrows an old order merely to submit to a new tyranny, who opens his bedroom to a so-called sexual enlightenment that merely replaces the antisexual morality of the Christian West. This type of man, intoxicated by alleged sexual revolution and freedom, ignores the fact that he is not truly mature. He remains incapable of thinking and acting independently. He has removed old pressures only to surrender to new ones. There is one difference: In the past the antisexual morality of the Churches established the norms of sexual attitude, while their role today has been taken over by the sexual "enlightenment specialist" or by open or secret pornographers.

The ethic of success, essential for achievement in profession and society, contributes to the situation that enables Christian morality and its antagonism to sex to coexist with this alleged sexual revolution. Whoever adheres to the success ethic surrenders to pressures of bourgeois morality that demand a "correct" and "respectable" life, which limits the response to sexual needs to marriage while creating pressures toward sexual activity, just as demanded by the so-called sexual revolution. This schizophrenic situation profits those who turn sexuality into a commercial product, as well as all those who owe their political, economic and social success to a pattern which demands that man say one thing, mean another and do a third.

Mature man uses all available methods to struggle

against the success ethic because this "ethic" is a dangerous instrument of the ruling institution. His ethic must
be one of responsibility. This means that he has to be
responsible for all results of his actions.[7] Neither *ex
cathedra* rulings nor the success such rulings promise decide his thought and action. He thinks and acts in such a
way that he can always bear the responsibility for what
he does. Thus, his sex life does not obey the rules of bourgeois morality within the so-called Christian West but
those of his own convictions. He must be convinced of his
own faith, his own salvation[8] and everything he regards
as divine. He must achieve a manner of harmonizing this
conviction with his sexual needs so that he need not be
concerned with what others say or regard as proper, but
he must always be concerned that his sexual life does
not harm someone else. Above all, he keeps in mind that
the conception of children is an act of prime human responsibility. Whoever conceives children but cannot
achieve a joyful life, commits the greatest imaginable
crime.

25. Religion and Sexuality

Mature man seeks to discover what is true and right. Immature man only cares to know whatever truths are fashionable and dominant in his society. The mature Christian, concerned with religion and sexuality, seeks to satisfy his sexual needs responsibly and on the basis of personal religious convictions. By contrast, immature man molds his sexual life to placate the morality of his rulers. He conforms to the ethic of success.

When we state that mature man's life is based on personal religious convictions and experiences, the question may be asked whether religion and sexuality are at all mutually acceptable. This book has, I believe, shown convincingly that many religions support the thesis that religion and sexuality are not antagonists but are life forces that can supplement each other. I should like to strengthen this thesis still further. In particular, I wish to counter possible allegations that the examples I have chosen from various religions refer only to the relationship between sexuality and specific religions, not to relations between sex and religion as a whole.

In order to deal successfully with such arguments, I

should like to answer the following questions: What main characteristics of religion are common to *all* religions? What relations do the main characteristics of religion have to man, specifically the elimination of evil? Do the main characteristics of religion demand that man ignore sexual needs in favor of religion? Is the rift between religious man (*homo religiosus*) and sexual man (*homo sexologicus*) a source of salvation or evil?

II

Definitions of religion are without number. That alone shows religion to be a life force that cannot be precisely defined. Nor can religion be encompassed and described in quantitative terms. We have, therefore, not attempted a new definition of religion.[1] But we must keep one thing in mind. Any definition of religion is useless that does not acknowledge as phenomena of religion the moments of experience, encounter and response that manifest themselves in action. Thus, religion is simultaneously a subjective personal experience and an objective reality. Under the impact of a sociology that surrendered itself to empiricism, religion has been defined as mere objective reality; but this conveys little of the actual phenomena of religion.

Among the basic characteristics of religion and religiosity is man's conviction that there exist powerful elements within him, beside him and above him, which he cannot command, although they influence his faith decisively. These he must venerate and serve in order to achieve and maintain salvation. Man's relations to these matters may be either passive, active, positive or negative; they satisfy his need for contact with an irrational and supernatural world he regards as quite different from the immediate, rationally approachable world around him. It would seem practical for man to view these supernatural powers, which he is incapable of describing, as something totally separate. They could be separate and different in a variety of ways. If man believes in the soul-nature of things (animism), in non-corporeal entities (ghosts) as a secret force (irrational might), or in the existence of several higher beings who usually have personal characteristics (polytheism), then we deal with the experience of something totally different and separate; but if he believes in a personal God (monotheism), then we deal with a different thing as such.

Therefore, while there are many religions, all have some things in common that enable us to speak of religion as a whole. This belief in a different reality, whether holy or sacred, separates it from the profane or non-sacred reality. Within a holy reality we encounter something incorporating supernatural "forces," be it time, space, man, animal or inanimate object. The most important and decisive role, however, is inherent in the "force" itself and in its manifestations. The experience of holy reality follows the decisive moment of man's encounter with it, either immediate (as in a vision) or intermediate (through various channels). These experiences and encounters result in a need to take action in the religious and sacred or in the profane area.

While it is legitimate to differentiate between the sacred and profane areas of life, a division between them is impossible. Religious action manifests itself in the sacred area, as in a cult, while the profane area is the setting for social action. Max Weber has cited ascetic Protestantism as a valid example. Experience, encounter and response are major characteristics of religion; content, fulfillment, depth of encounter with the divine and an appropriate response or action which this encounter prompts are decisive to the nature of various religions.

III

Sexuality, in our context,[2] includes everything concerned with the satisfaction of needs that result from the fact that man is a sexual being. The results of this satisfaction (including pregnancy and venereal diseases) are not identical with the sexual; they must therefore be regarded separately. This difference between sex and its results emerges from existing data of an anthropological, ethnological, sociological and religio-scientific nature. We note that man originally did not find that his encounter with the divine disturbed sexual needs or their satisfactions. His religious experiences were often so closely linked with sex that it was difficult to separate the two life forces of religion and sexuality. Man experienced his first religiously linked anxiety concerning sex as the *result* of the sexual; in particular, masculine society faces such fears when it encounters menstruation, pregnancy and birth. For this reason, the original religiously oriented laws and taboos did not concern sexual life as such, but sought to limit dangers concerning the results of sex. Harmony between religious and sexual experiences was not threatened by sex but its results.

This harmony was disturbed whenever masculine society isolated itself from feminine society so that only a relation of dependence could exist between the two sexes. Where masculine society seeks to rule over women, woman is seen as man's property, and the female sex is identified with evil. Masculine society succeeded in overcoming its archaic fears of the opposite sex when it saw woman not only as causing the results of sex but as the

very epitome of sex, which had to be isolated and de-
feated. As long as man listened to the voice of nature—
regardless of any denigration or enslavement of women
—he was able to experience religion and sex as two elements that could get along with each other. But the voice
of nature was drowned out by the voices of philosophers
who disrupted any harmony between the religious and
sexual experience, a disruption that had begun with the
downgrading of woman and ended with her removal from
the Divine area.

As long as man experienced religion and sexuality spontaneously and was able to come to terms with both, there
could be no rift between these two life forces. The major
characteristics of religion—experience, encounter and response—harmonized with the satisfaction of sexual need;
this has not only been true for so-called primitive peoples
but in other population groups as well, or wherever religion remains untouched by dualistic concepts. The major characteristics of religion do not contain elements of
discord between religion and sex. Rather, it is the content
of several religions or the teaching of several philosophers
(including religious men) who asked for a decision between religion and sexuality. This becomes clearer still
when we remember our analysis of the various main characteristics of religious thoughts and actions.

IV

We have already noted[3] that National Religion is con-
ditioned by broadly representing folk religion (as in ancient Rome) and not merely the concepts of an isolated
social structure; further, salvation could be reached
within this framework of ideas. By contrast, a Universal
Religion is essentially a religion of individuals: The indi-

vidual is a bearer of religious responsibility who encounters evil rather than salvation. By this encounter with the world, which becomes the subject of his rational insight and conscious creation, he looks for appropriate ways of overcoming evil. It is thus possible that the individual will seek salvation within a collective, which, in contrast with the original collective (folk religion), may be categorized as a folk faith. We deal here with "mass religiosity" supported by an unstructured multiplicity whose main characteristics are formed by a primitive structure of religious thoughts and feelings.

Within this context, we encounter forms designed to remove evil and actions closely linked with whatever has been experienced or recognized as such evil. Within the folk religions and within the framework of traditions that have emerged from it, the individual's isolation from the group is regarded as evil and can be removed by adherence to the appropriate group; possibilities and forms of actions are limited by a man's total dependence on his group. Universal religions enable the individual to determine the content and form of evil; he may seek salvation outside the group because everyone experiences and recognizes his fate in personal terms. Strong personalities who appear as charismatic leaders and/or teachers become founders of religions and of philosophical concepts that promise salvation, or its realization, as experienced and recognized by the founder.

The Christian religion has the special characteristic that the individual eliminates evil, on the basis of his encounter with Christ and his teachings, as he is freed from all compulsions and controls. Response to such an encounter is a personal action as the individual uses all his powers voluntarily to achieve a renewal and re-creation of world and society within the meaning of Christ. The world, cre-

ated through specific Christian thought and action, enables one to act independently of social and other
background, because the individual himself is of supreme
value. All other values, be they material or spiritual, serve
only to help man in his efforts to unfold his personality,
free of all compulsions. Finally, a Christian world can
only be a world based on the power of love, the reconciliation of man with God, with nature, with himself and
his fellow man.

V

As long as man responds to folk-religiosity, the group
to which he belongs offers him an opportunity of partici-
pating in the material things it controls. Among these is
the satisfaction of human needs that result from his iden-
tity as a sexual being. In most folk religions, sex is regarded as a creative force that affirms the origin of life,
inseparable from all other areas of existence, part of the
mytho-religious elements that permeate all of man's life.
Man experiences as a group member and through his folk-
religiosity, that sex is a gift of the gods and of nature,
often identical with life itself and thus of a blessing bestowed upon his group. He regards sexuality as evil only
when its results disturb the group's harmonious existence.
This is not caused by a morality that might put a low
value on the body or on sex. Group harmony is only disturbed when specific events insult the gods or the patriarchal structure of the collective. This can happen when
someone violates some magical, but not "morally" motivated, taboo, or when one man ignores the property rights
of another or intrudes upon his sphere of interests.

The question of sexuality in man's efforts to counter
personal evil arises only within the Universal Religions,

where man has to achieve salvation on the basis of a personal choice that often forces him to separate himself from his environment. Where this environment is regarded as a source of evil, it calls for the removal of an evil situation that may run counter to the social environment and its value systems. Wherever the environment and its values are regarded as a divine gift, the individual seeks to structure his environment so that it will aid him in overcoming evil.

Whenever man excludes the "worldly" from the sphere of the sacred, he seeks to achieve salvation by overcoming material values and by spiritualizing his life. It is possible, under these circumstances, that men and women who regard their bodies as antagonistic to the spiritual, will turn against sex as a dangerous enemy of religion and, therefore, as a source of evil. This is particularly likely wherever the satisfaction of sexual needs, as well as the satisfaction of religious needs, demand man's total surrender. This competition between religious and sexual devotion is both cause and effect of a rift between religion and sex, which exists only in Universal Religions with dualistic ideas. Universal Religions that do not know Dualism, such as Islam, affirm the sexual as a source of pleasure and make it part of their plan for salvation.

Christianity may ideally be seen as a Universal Religion that does not specifically favor either Dualism or the Satanization of the body or of sex. On the one hand, Christ eliminates all contradictions, seeking to reconcile man with God, with himself, his own nature and his fellow men; he also teaches us that Christ can eliminate situations of evil through unhesitating belief in Christ. This faith achieves man's own total liberation, eliminating all compulsions and controls, and enables him to restructure the "world" into a source of joy for all mankind. Pierre

Teilhard de Chardin writes correctly that Christianity is not an additional burden of exercises and duties that add still more to the heavy burden of the community or to already severely restricting rules and regulations. He says: "Christianity is, in fact, one powerfully acting soul which contributes fresh meaning, magic, and a new serenity to our own actions."[4]

Among the most important factors that would make life appear as a beautiful adventure, rather than a burden, are, in addition to unrestricted faith in Christ, the fruits of this faith, such as freedom, justice, peace, humanity and love, as well as human progress in technology, based on independent human thought and action; all these are outgrowths of Christian faith.

As long as such progress serves man, it should be viewed as God's gift, designed to help man in his efforts to eliminate a situation of evil. Among these gifts are harmless methods enabling man to satisfy his sexual needs without concern about results. Safe separation of the sex act from its results, combined with responsible control over the results of sexuality with due respect for genuine Christian value—love above all—can in a truly Christian society lead to total removal of doubt from the sexual. This can remove all negative reactions to the results of man's sexual functions.

It is not easy to speak of Christian love in a context of sexuality because the concept of love has been so totally misused and debased; at the same time hidden and open pornography have made "love-making" synonymous with "coitus." Still, Jiddu Krishnamurti[5] is right when he says, "Where there is love, sex is never a problem—it is the lack of love that creates the problem." We should not, however, see Christian love as an emotional entity. Particularly in the case of sexuality, Christian love remains, we should remember, a rational force. In my opinion, Christian love means man's ability always to consider whether one's actions are likely to harm someone else or whether, to put it in positive terms, one helps others in their effort to overcome evil.

A passionate young man who tells a girl, "I love you," may consciously or unconsciously use "love" to disguise mere desire and passion. Once he has satisfied himself, he may pay no attention to the results of such "love." Whoever loves in a Christian sense, sees to it that the results of his sexual activity harm no one. Seen in this way, Christian love achieves much more than all the rules put together that seek to regulate man's sex life through legislation and taboos. Finally, as we understand Christian love, it gives a totally new meaning to such concepts as matrimony, marriage and family.

Matrimony, marriage and family do not exist to legalize or satisfy temporary emotions or passions; rather, they constantly remind man that he bears lasting responsibility for the results of his sexual life—specifically for any human life he creates and places into this world. The most important and possibly only task of Christian morality and ethic should, under these conditions, be the enlightenment of contemporary mankind, particularly youth, urging it to satisfy its sexual needs in a manner that does no damage. This, however, assumes that educators learn to separate sexuality from its results; it assumes unrestricted affirmation of sex and of the enjoyment it provides.

VI

The so-called Christian West suffers from the exploitation of sexual problems for criminal purposes and the en-

richment of those who profit from the sexual needs of
their fellow men. We are, in my opinion, paying the price
for the results of an Original Sin and Inherited Sin, forcing the young generation to pay for sins they inherited
from an older generation. Today's mankind has to pay
the price for centuries-old sins of theologians and
Churches, men who issued innumerable laws that turned
a traditionally joyful message into a burden, that prevented man from lifting himself out of a situation of evil.

It was, in particular, so-called Christian morality—
which, as we have seen, emerged from non-Christian, pagan and dualistic concepts of man—that prompted a
separation between Christianity and sex, turning both into
sources of evil. Instead of a Christocentric and anthropocentric ethic, it imposed a genitocentric morality which
in many ways destroyed Christ's work. Love was replaced
by law, allied to antagonists of genuine Christian values
in order to retain its power. Elimination of conflicts, the
reconciliation of man with God, with his nature, with
himself and his fellow man was replaced by new contradictions and animosities that had been unknown, to this
degree, within the non-Christian or pre-Christian world;
in particular, it caused animosity between man and
woman in the service of Christian morality. Freedom was
replaced by total dominance of men over men that could
function, and still functions, in the Christian West because theologians and Churches invented a sexual
morality that permitted total control over man, his submission to varieties of repression.

We have noted that when viewed in a world or society
that calls itself Christian, man is supremely valuable.
Whether an ethical principle may call itself Christian or
not, depends on whether man is truly a psychosomatic
being to be healed bodily and spiritually, and thus made

free. A morality that causes suffering is un-Christian. Therefore, the so-called Christian sexual ethic has no connection with Christ's teachings, is of pagan origin and has created nothing but suffering. The history of the Christian West, as seen in the daily press, is filled with crimes committed in the name of morality.

Among the suffering that Christian morality has caused are, in particular, the identification of woman with evil, her resulting degradation and enslavement, and the departure of youth from an institutionalized Christianity it regards as opposed to a natural, joyful and happy existence. But hope is now justified that the young generation has become convinced that man does not live by bread or sex alone, and that it may, more than previous generations, become involved with such genuine Christian values as love, justice, freedom and peace—in short, with humanism. In a world that may emerge from such an involvement, there can no longer be room for an antisexual, and therefore antihuman, morality within the Churches.

NOTES

I. RELIGION AND SEXUALITY

1. Origins of Sexual Pleasure

1. New York, 1933.

2. Quoted in Hays, Hoffman R., *The Dangerous Sex: The Myth of Feminine Evil* (New York, 1964).

3. See De Rachewiltz, Boris, whose volume on sexual customs in Africa, past and present, was originally published in Italy under the title *Eros Nero* (*Black Eros*) and is also available in a German translation.

4. Medicine men are primitive witch doctors whose main function is healing. They exercise their healing skills by parapsychological means, using well-guarded techniques.

5. The writings of Margaret Mead, including her well-known *Growing Up in Samoa,* provide much valuable data. Her combined studies on youth and sexuality in primitive societies were published under the title, *From the South Seas* (New York, 1939). While much of this material has become outdated in historic anthropological terms because of the rapid modernization of the areas in question, its significance to the relationship between religion and sexuality remains valid.

6. See Note 3.

7. The original German title of the Lommel volume is *Fortschritt ins Nichts.* It deals with the modernization of the Australian aborigines. The author is indebted to Lommel for additional data used in this chapter.

8. See Note 3.

2. *Toward Sexual Harmony*

1. The reader is referred to *The Dangerous Sex* by Hays for additional data.
2. The author has drawn on the Hays volume, which cites *Head-Hunters of Papua*, by Tony Saulnier (New York, 1968).
3. Papua shields have been decorated with drawings that show prone men with heads placed between their legs (Hays; Saulnier).
4. Hays cites *Stone Men of Malekula*, by John W. Layard (London, 1942).
5. As previously cited, writings by Mead; see also, Malinowski, Bronislaw, *Sex and Repression in Savage Society* (New York, 1927).
6. Reich, Wilhelm, *Der Einbruch der Sexualmoral* (Copenhagen, 1931).
7. Concerning Eskimo religiosity, see Lantis, M., *Alaskan Eskimo Ceremonialism*, Monographs of the American Ethnological Society, II (New York, 1947). Also, specifically, Nansen, Fridtjof, *Eskimo Life* (London, 1893).
8. Nansen, F.
9. Frazer, James G., *The Golden Bough* (London, 1960; as well as numerous earlier and subsequent editions). Further, van der Leeuw, G., *Phänomenologie der Religion* (Tübingen, 1956): "As a revelation of power, every birth represents a miracle" (p. 212).
10. Schubart, Walter, *Religion und Eros* (Munich, 1941): "When man encountered the Enigma of Woman, he faced two religious alternatives. He could either place her in particularly close relation to the Divinity, or he could view her as suspect of contact with demons" (p. 187).
11. Thus, Horney, Karen, "The Dread of Women," in *International Journal of Psychoanalysis*, Vol. 13 (London, 1932).

3. *The Gods of Love*

1. Equivalent to accelerated sexual drive, notably in pathological form.
2. Equivalent to means designed to increase or provoke sexual desire.
3. See von Wilamowitz-Mollendorff, Ulrich, *Der Glaube der Hellenen* (Darmstadt, 1955).

Notes

. Frickenhaus, as cited by von Wilamowitz-Mollendorf.

5. Ling, Trevor, *A History of Religion in East and West* (New York, 1968).

6. Concerning the religion of the Greeks, see Rohde, Erwin, *Psyche* (New York, 1966).

7. Among contemporary sources, Schneider, C. and Rumpf, A., in *Reallexikon für Antike und Christentum* (Stuttgart, 1964).

8. Hesiod, *Theogony.*

9. Plato's *The Symposium* has been variously translated; one translation was made by the English poet Percy B. Shelley (Chicago, 1895).

10. The word's origin is "tribo," Greek for "rubbing," from which derives "tribadism," equivalent to lesbian relations, or female homosexuality.

11. Plato's *Symposium.*

12. See Licht, Hans, *Sexual Life in Ancient Greece* (London, 1932).

13. See works by Licht, Nilsson, Otto, etc.

14. Hesiod, *Theogony.*

15. Plato's *Symposium.*

4. Cults of the Phallus

1. In addition to Hans Licht's book, cited in the preceding chapter, see Vorberg, G., *Glossarium Eroticum* (Hanau, 1965).

2. Concerning the following data, see Licht.

3. Licht.

4. Homer, *Odyssey* (various translations and editions).

5. For this reason, the chastity belt is also known as the "Florentine Belt."

6. Herter, H., *De Priapo* (Berlin, 1932); Buchheit, V., *Studien zum Corpus Priapeorum* (1952).

7. Among English-language sources: Scott, R. G., *Phallic Worship* (London, 1941); Gaster, H. T., *Ritual, Myth and Drama in the Ancient Near East* (New York, 1950). Also, previously cited works by De Rachewiltz and Schubart.

8. Licht.

9. Ibid.

10. Ibid.

11. Ibid.

12. De Rachewiltz.

13. See Guthrie, W., *Orpheus and Greek Religion* (London, 1952).

14. Wilamowitz-Moellendorff.

15. The concept *Stoa* originated with Zenon's habit of meeting with his students in the *soa poikile* (hall of pillars) in Athens. See Mates, B., *Stoic Logic* (Berkeley, 1935).

16. Sources are numerous, including: Arnou, R., *De platonismo Patrum* (Rome, 1935); Danielou, I., *Platonisme et théologie mystique* (Paris, 1934); Hoffmann, E., *Platonismus und christliche Philosophie* (Zurich, 1960); Jaeger, W., *Early Christianity and Greek Paideia* (Cambridge, 1962).

17. Plotin (pp. 204–270); major creator of Neoplatonism.

5. Religion and Sex in Harmony

1. See Maspéro, H., "Les prodédeés de 'nourrir l'esprit vital' dans la religion taoiste ancienne," *Journal Asiatique* (April-June and July-September 1937).

2. *Kama Sutra*. This book on Indian love techniques is available in a variety of translations.

3. The author has been unable to trace this quote, found among his notes, to its source.

4. See Sasaki, G.: "The Indian Attitude towards Morality," *France-Asie*, 193 (1968).

5. The Koran, or The Holy Qu-ran, numerous translations and editions.

6. Ibid.

7. See Pickthall, M. M., *The Meaning of the Glorious Koran* (New York, 1954).

8. *The Perfumed Garden of Sheik Nefzaoui* (London, 1886).

9. *Tales of One Thousand and One Nights*, widely popular since first introduced to Western readers in a French translation by Antoine Galland, an archaeologist (Paris, 1704–17).

10. *The Perfumed Garden of Sheik Nefzaoui*.

11. The Koran.

12. From a report on Afghanistan in the German periodical *Die Zeit* (November 27, 1970).

13. Sura 2 of the Koran: "She will endanger you; therefore, do

not approach her during the monthly purification, and do not go near them until they are purified."

14. Book of Kings 11:3.

15. Deuteronomy 24:5.

16. See Bailey, Derrick Sherwin, *Sexual Relations in Christian Thought* (New York, 1959).

17. Whereas the Ten Commandments state, "Thou shalt not commit adultery," Deuteronomy 21:11 permits a man who "seest among the captives a beautiful woman and hast a desire unto her" to take her as "thy wife." If he finds "no delight in her, then thou shalt let her go whither she will."

18. Ecclesiastes 7:26.

19. See Leviticus 7:6 or Deuteronomy 6:20.

20. See Exodus 22:16; Deuteronomy 22:13; Leviticus 21:14.

21. Bailey.

22. Cited from *The Song of Songs,* translated into German (*Das Lied der Lieder*) and annotated by Leopold Marx (Stuttgart, 1964).

II. RELIGION AGAINST SEXUALITY

6. Christianity and Sex

1. See Savramis, Demosthenes, *Entchristlichung und Sexualisierung: Zwei Vorurteile* (Munich, 1969).

2. Concerning the following, see Savramis, *Theologie und Gesellschaft* (Munich, 1971).

3. II Corinthians 5:17.

4. II Corinthians 3:17.

5. Mark 2:27.

6. In addition to the above-noted works of the author, see also, Savramis, "Wertsysteme in traditionalen und industriellen Gesellschaften," *Internationales Jahrbuch für Religionssoziologie*, Vol. 6 (1970).

7. Matthew 5:27, 28, "Ye have heard that it was said by them of old time, 'Thou shalt not commit adultery. But I say unto you, That whosoever looketh on a woman to lust after her hath committed adultery with her already in his heart." Also, Matthew 5:31, 32: "It hath been said, 'Whosoever shall put away his wife, let him give her a writing of divorcement. But I say unto you, That

whosoever shall put away his wife, saving for the cause of fornica-
tion, causeth her to commit adultery; and whosoever shall marry
her that is divorced committeth adultery." Further, Matthew 19:3;
Mark 12:18–25; Matthew 22:22–33; Luke 20:27–38 and John
8:3–11.

8. Bailey, *Sexual Relations.*

9. Particularly, Matthew 19:3–10 and Mark 10:1–12.

10. Deuteronomy 24:1–4.

11. Mark 10:7, 8.

12. Matthew 5:27.

13. John 8:3–11.

14. Leviticus 20:10.

15. See Schalom Ben-Chorin's work *Bruder Jesus* (*Brother Jesus*),
a Jewish view of the Nazarene (Munich, 1967); notably concerning
Jesus and women.

16. See Mark 10:6 and Matthew 19:4.

17. Luke 8:1–3.

18. John 11:5.

19. John 4:27. William E. Phipps maintains in *Was Jesus Married?*
(New York, 1971) that Jesus was most probably married. Ben-
Chorin (see Note 15) assumes that Jesus must have been married,
as his disciples addressed him as "Rabbi," and an unmarried Rabbi
is unthinkable.

7. *Theology and Sex*

1. Concerning the following, see also Savramis, *Theologie und
Gesellschaft.*

2. II Corinthians 5:14; Ephesians 6:24; I Corinthians 16:22.

3. Romans 8:35; II Timothy 1:7.

4. Colossians 3:15; 2:6, 7; Romans 1:21; I Thessalonians 5:8; Romans 14:6, 7; I Timothy 4:3.

5. Romans 8:28.

6. Ephesians 4:2; Philippians 2:3; Colossians 3:12; I Corinthians
15:10 and 3:5.

7. I Thessalonians 5:17; Colossians 4:2; Ephesians 6:18.

8. Romans 13:8; Galatians 5:14.

9. Colossians 3:14.

10. Galatians 5:15.

11. II Timothy 3:1.

12. I Corinthians 13:8.
13. Galatians 6:1 ff.; I Corinthians 13:5.
14. Ephesians 4:2; Romans 14:1; I Corinthians 13:4.
15. I Thessalonians 5:14 ff.
16. Galatians 6:2.
17. I Corinthians 13:5; see also I Corinthians 10:33: "Even as I please all men in all things, not seeking mine own profit, but the profit of many, that they may be saved."
18. *Die Mystik des Apostel Paulus* (Tübingen, 1930).
19. I Corinthians 13. See also, Harnack, A., *Das Hohe Lied des Apostel Paulus von der Liebe und seine religionsgeschichtliche Bedeutung* (1911); also Nygrem and others.
20. "And though I have all faith . . . and have not charity, I am nothing."
21. I Corinthians 13:4–7. Love is essential to all social life (Galatians 6:9, 10; I Corinthians 16:4; Ephesians 5:2 and 4:32). Paul endeavors so that all Christians be "rooted and grounded in love" (Ephesians 3:17).
22. II Corinthians 3:17.
23. I Corinthians 7:1.
24. I Corinthians 7:9.
25. I Corinthians 7:2.
26. I Corinthians 7:2–4.
27. See Buber, Martin, *I and Thou.*
28. I Corinthians 7:38.
29. Ben-Chorin, Schalom: *Paulus, der Wanderapostel in jüdischer Sicht* (Munich, 1970); a Jewish view of Paul.
30. Galatians 3:28.
31. I Corinthians 11:3.
32. I Corinthians 11:7.
33. Ibid.
34. I Corinthians 7:25.
35. I Corinthians 13:7.
36. Galatians 5:1.
37. Klausner, Joseph, *Von Jesus zu Paulus* (Jerusalem, 1950).
38. II Corinthians 12:7.
39. Stern, Arthur, "Zum Problem der Epilepsie des Paulus," *Psychiatria et Neurologia*, Vol. 133, No. 5 (Basle, 1957).
40. I Corinthians 7:29.
41. I Corinthians 7:31.

42. I Corinthians 7:9.

43. For an initial orientation in bibliographical sources concerning Augustine, see Marrou, Henri, *Augustinus in Selbsterzeugnissen und Bilddokumenten* (Reinbek, 1965).

44. For example, Augustine, *De nup. et concup.* I, 6.

45. *The Confessions of St. Augustine;* various translations and editions.

46. Augustine, *De gratia Christi de peccato originale*, 2, 40.

47. Augustine, *De nup. et concup.* I, 8.

8. Church and Sex

1. See also, Savramis, *Theologie und Gesellschaft* (Munich, 1971).

2. Concerning the Byzantine Church and theology, see Beck, Hans Georg, *Kirche und theologische Literatur im byzantinischen Reich* (Munich, 1959).

3. Biographical data in Savramis, *Zur Soziologie des byzantinischen Mönchtums* (Leyden-Cologne, 1962).

4. Savramis, "Max Webers Beitrag zum besseren Verständnis der ostkirchlichen 'ausserweltlichen' Askese," in Max Weber zum Gedächtnis, Sonderheft 7 der *Kölner Zeitschrift für Soziologie und Sozialpsychologie*, pp. 334–58 (Cologne and Opladen, 1963).

5. De Mendieta, E. A., *La prèsqu'ile des Caloyers: Le mont Athos* (Paris, 1955) contains bibliography concerning Athos.

6. Savramis, "Die religiösen Grundlagen der neu-griechischen Gesellschaft," *Die verhinderte Demokratie: Modell Griechenland* (Frankfurt, 1969).

7. Nissiotis, Nikos, *Die Theologie der Ostkirche im ökumenischen Dialog* (Stuttgart, 1968).

8. Concerning the Orthodox view of man, Russian and Greek sources provide a variety of aspects.

9. Bratsiotis, P., *Die Lehre der orthodoxen Kirche über die Theosis des Menschen* (Brussels, 1961).

10. See previously noted works by Savramis.

11. Michel, A., *Die Kaisermacht der Ostkirche, 843–1204* (Darmstadt, 1959).

12. Savramis, previously noted.

13. To the Orthodox believer, the divine qualities of reason, liberty and love have been weakened, although not made powerless, by sin. Therefore, his sexual life should develop more constructively

than that of someone whose view of man forces him to see himself as totally depraved by sin.

14. As noted in the writings of Savramis, the Eastern Church's view of man opens two possibilities. One points toward man's effort toward the renewal of the individual and of society, on the basis of God's will; i.e., an active and socially oriented Christianity. The other remains an egotistic and one-sided effort to achieve fulfillment, strictly for oneself in solitude, leading toward a passive, asocial or even antisocial Christianity. The second road embodies a negative view of the world and its values, whereas the first grows from the optimistic outlook that man is capable of self-renewal, enlightenment, and even divine achievement.

15. The concept of divine achievement has influenced thought and action among Eastern Christianity, be it in the Russian Church, Greece or the Eastern cults of Roman Catholicism.

16. See Note 1.

17. Grabmann, M., *Mittelalterliches Geistesleben* (Munich, 1926); Van Steenberghen, F., *Aristotle in the West* (Louvain, 1951).

18. Van Steenberghen, F., *Philosophie des Mittelalters* (Bern, 1950).

19. Schmölz, F.-M., "Thomas von Aquin," *Staatslexikon der Görres-Gesellschaft*, Vol. 7 (Freiburg, 1962).

20. De Vries, W., *Orthodoxie und Katholizismus* (Freiburg, 1965).

21. *Cleros* (from which "clerical" derives) means "lot" in Greek. As the Apostles were chosen by lot, it originally referred to the total community of the faithful. In the second century, the meaning became restricted to those who officiated at churchly rites.

22. *Abhandlungen zur Philosophie, Psychologie und Pädagogik*, Vol. 17 (Bonn, 1969).

23. Thomas Aquinas, *Summa Theologica*.

24. Ibid.

25. Meinhold, Peter, *Konzile der Kirche in evangelischer Sicht* (Stuttgart, 1962).

26. Beginning February 10, 1880.

27. Beginning December 31, 1930.

28. Bibliographical data will be found in Notes concerning the chapter dealing with "*Humanae Vitae* and Its Critics."

29. Messenger, E. C., *Two in One Flesh* (London, 1948).

30. Hopfenbeck, G., *Jugendbeichte* (dealing with confessions by youths). Companion volumes by the same author deal with con-

fessions by adult men and women (all, Augsburg, 1964, 1968, 1969).

31. Schwenger, H., *Antisexualle Propaganda* (Heidelberg, 1971).

32. Luke 10:25 ff.

9. *The Satanization of Women*

1. Reference should be made to the penis-envy concept of Sigmund Freud. Further, Friedan, Betty, *The Feminine Mystique* (New York, 1969).

2. Mark 10:6 and Matthew 19:4.

3. Galatians 3:28.

4. I Corinthians 11:7; I Corinthians 11:3.

5. As quoted in Leclerque, J. David, *Die Familie: Ein Handbuch* (Freiburg, 1958).

6. Ibid.

7. *De cult. fem.* I, I.

8. See Savramis, *Enchristlichung und Sexualisierung: Zwei Vorurteile* (Munich, 1969).

9. Baroja, C. J., *The World of Witches* (Chicago, 1964); Hansen, Joseph, *Zauberwahn, Inquisition und Hexenprozess im Mittelalter und die Entstehung der grossen Hexenverfolgung* (Leipzig, 1900).

10. "The total number of deaths in Europe cannot be accurately estimated; careful evaluations vary between several hundred thousand and one million," Baschwitz, Kurt, *Hexen und Hexenprozesse* (Munich, 1966).

11. According to Baschwitz: "The Inquisitor Institoris had been given the opportunity, by the Konstanz Diocese, to torture and burn women. His fellow member of the Order, Jakob Sprenger, Cologne professor of theology, joined him. Institoris arranged witch trials in the town of his birth, Schlettstadt (Alsace) and in several other towns; he continued to call them trials of heretics. His victims, tortured, in pain and fear of death, had to testify to everything their tormentors wanted to hear. These so-called confessions were used by the two inquisitors to prove the existence of an immense witch conspiracy."

12. Sprenger, Jacobus and Institoris, Henricus, *Malleus Maleficarum* (Lyon, 1584).

13. Baschwitz.

14. *Malleus Maleficarum.*

15. Bolen, Carl Van, *Geschichte der Erotik* (Munich, 1966).

16. Englisch, P., *Geschichte der erotischen Literatur* (Stuttgart, 1932).

17. Concerning the papal Bulls of 1434 and 1484, see Hansen, Joseph.

18. II Corinthians 5:17.

19. See Encyclical *Casti Connubi,* as cited in *Humanae Vitae.*

20. As cited in *Publik* (German periodical), May 8, 1970.

10. Celibacy

1. Kottje, Raymund, "Zur Geschichte des Zölibatwesens," *Ehelosogkeit des Priesters in Geschichte und Gegenwart* (Regensburg, 1970).

2. Ben-Chorin writes, "An unmarried Rabbi is unthinkable" (in *Bruder Jesus,* cited above) and adds that the Talmud denounced the unmarried state: "Whoever is without a wife is without joy, blessing or happiness . . . without peace. A man without a woman is not a full person."

3. De Rachewiltz.

4. Frazer, James G., *The Golden Bough.*

5. Ibid.

6. Ibid.

7. Erman, Adolf, *Die Religion der Ägypter* (Leipzig, 1934; Berlin, 1968).

8. Ibid.

9. Refer to Chapter 3, "The Gods of Love."

10. For bibliography, consult Kottje, R.

11. Ibid.

12. Ibid.

13. Note sixth canon of the Sixth Ecumenical Council.

14. See previously cited literature, in particular Savramis, "Das Konzildekret über den Apostolat der Laien und der Berücksichtigung der Stellung der Laien in der griechischorthodoxen Kirche," in *Kyrios,* Vol. 8 (1968).

15. Wach, Joachim, *Religionssoziologie* (Tübingen, 1951).

16. Savramis, *Die soziale Stellung der Priester in Griechenland* (Leyden, 1968).

17. Denzler, Georg, "Priesterehe und Priesterzölibat in historischer Sicht," *Existenzprobleme des Priesters* (Munich, 1969).

18. Theiner, Johann-Anton and Augustin, *Die Einführung der er-zwungenen Ehelosigkeit bei den christlichen Geistlichen und ihre Folgen* (Barmen, 1891).

19. Rost, H., *Die Katholiken im Kultur- und Wirtschaftsleben der Gegenwart* (Cologne, 1908).

20. ". . . and there be eunuchs for the kingdom of heaven's sake. *He that is able to receive it, let him receive it.*" (Author's emphasis.)

21. I Corinthians 7:1–7, in particular 7:6.

22. Author's emphasis.

23. See letter by the Bishop of Augsburg, Joseph Stimpfle, January 12, 1969.

24. Encyclical *Sacerdotalis Caelibatus,* June 24, 1967.

25. Ibid.

26. Art. 21.

III. SEXUALITY AGAINST RELIGION

11. *The Reformation Did Not Take Place*

1. Bernath, Klaus, *Anima Forma Corporis* (Bonn, 1969). The author notes correctly that "the ideas expressed by Thomas are based on a concealed fear of woman."

2. Bibliographical data may be found in Lilje, Hans, *Luther* (Reinbek, 1965).

3. The Reformation freed man because it linked his conscience directly to God.

4. See Luther, Martin, *Kommentar zum Galaterbrief* (his comments regarding "Galatians"), issued in 1519.

5. Ibid, Preamble.

6. Luther was unable to avoid the typical dilemma encountered by the monks of his period. See Erikson, Erik H., *Young Man Luther* (New York, 1958).

7. Note also Cole, William Graham, *Sex in Christianity and Psychoanalysis* (New York, 1955).

8. Luther speaks out against celibacy at various times, including his *Smalcaldian Letter* (1537), where he states ". . . we shall not agree to their despicable celibacy, and shan't permit it, but shall give free access to marriage, as God ordered and bestowed it. . . ."

9. Luther, *Complete Works.*

10. Ibid.

11. See sources cited in chapter on "Church and Sexuality."

12. See Savramis, *Entchristlichung;* also, Cole (see Note 7).

13. Calvin (1509–64).

14. Calvin, John, *Institutio Christianae Religionis.*

15. Ibid. Author's emphasis.

16. See also Gloede, G., *Theologia Naturalis bei Calvin* (Berlin, 1935).

17. Corpus Reformatorum, Vol. 29–87, *Johannis Calvini opera quae supersunt omnia* (Brunswick, 1863).

18. As cited by Bailey, D. S., *Sexual Relations in Christian Thought* (New York, 1959).

19. Luther, *Complete Works.*

20. Stricker, Käthe, *Die Frau in der Reformation* (Berlin, 1927).

21. As cited by Cole (see Note 7).

12. Marriage

1. Wingren, Gustav, *Luthers Lehre vom Beruf,* translated from the Swedish (Munich, 1952).

2. *The Confessions of St. Augustine;* references to "God's State."

3. Bernath, Klaus, *Anima Forma Corporis* (Bonn, 1969).

4. Note particularly, Levi-Strauss, Claude, *Les structures élémentaires de la parenté* (Paris, 1949).

5. Mead, Margaret, *From the South Seas* (New York, 1939).

6. Cole, *Sex in Christianity and Psychoanalysis.*

7. Ibid.

8. Note, for example, Engels, Friedrich, *Der Ursprung der Familie, des Privateigentums und des Staates* (Frankfurt, 1969) and Bebel, August, *Die Frau und der Sozialismus* (Berlin, 1964).

9. Bebel, ibid.

10. Thus, for instance, Arnold Gehlen, "The Social Structure of Primitive Societies" in *Soziologie* (Düsseldorf-Cologne, 1955).

11. Schelsky, Helmut, *Soziologie der Sexualität* (Hamburg, 1955).

12. Ibid.

13. Murdock, G. P., *Social Structure* (New York, 1949).

14. Ibid.

15. Ibid.

16. Gehlen, Arnold, "Die Sozialstruktur primitiver Gesellschaften," *Soziologie* (Düsseldorf, 1955).

17. See Hillman, Eugene, "Die Entwicklung christlicher Ehestrukturen," *Concilium*, 6 (1970).

18. Bibliographical data as provided by Hillman.

19. Barrett, David B., *Schism and Renewal in Africa* (Nairobi, 1968).

20. Hillman.

21. Paul VI, *Africae Terrarum* (October 1967).

22. Hillman.

13. Prostitution

1. Bernath, Klaus, *Anima Forma Corporis.*

2. Ibid.

3. Ibid.

4. Luther, *Complete Works.*

5. In addition to numerous German-language works, the author consulted Rolph, C. H. (ed.), *Woman of the Street: A Sociological Study of the Common Prostitute* (London, 1955).

6. The author has consulted Bebel's work in a recent edition, the 61st printing, published in Berlin in 1964.

7. Ibid.

8. De Rachewiltz.

9. Morus (pseud. of Richard Lewinsohn), *Eine Weltgeschichte der Sexualität* (Reinbek, 1956).

10. Saller, Karl, "Sexualität und Sitte in der vorindustriellen Zeit," in *Familie und Gesellschaft* (Tübingen, 1966).

11. Bauer, Willi, *Geschichte und Wesen der Prostitution* (Stuttgart, 1968).

12. Block, Iwan; cited by Bauer.

13. Evola, Julius (Giulio), *Metaphysik des Sexus,* translated from the Italian (Stuttgart, 1962).

14. Schubart, Walter, *Religion und Eros* (Munich, 1941).

15. Author's emphasis.

16. See also Savramis re: social position of priests in Greece; cited previously.

14. Pornography

1. By supplying her customers, Beate Uhse grossed 30.6 million Deutsche Mark (approximately 8 million dollars) in 1969, *Der Spiegel*, No. 32 (1970).

2. Ibid.

3. *Die Zeit* (November 21, 1969).

4. *Porne*=whore; *grapho*=writing.

5. Among the extensive literature, the author wishes to cite Mertner, Edgar and Mainusch, Herbert, *Pornotopia* (Frankfurt, 1970).

6. Interview in *Der Spiegel* with Dr. Hans Giese, No. 32 (1970).

7. See chapter on "Cults of the Phallus."

8. Licht, Hans, *Sittengeschichte Griechenlands* (Dresden and Zurich, 1925/28).

9. As quoted by Licht.

10. Ibid.

11. Ibid.

12. Savramis, *Entchristlichung und Sexualisierung;* cited previously.

13. Researchers have found that the customers of pornography are not predominantly those who, according to the antisexual "morality" of the Christian West, conduct themselves in an "immoral manner." This was shown in tests undertaken by James L. Howard at the University of North Carolina, Chapel Hill, in 1969. The young students involved became quickly satiated with sex films and pornographic publications; some refused to take the test a second time, saying that it was boring and poorly paid.

15. The So-called Sexual Revolution

1. The author dealt with this subject in a German-language work—Savramis, Demosthenes, *Entchristlichung und Sexualisierung: Zwei Vorurteile* (Munich, 1969).

2. Ibid.

3. Unless I am mistaken, the expression "sexual revolution" originated with Pitrim A. Sorokin, who wrote a book entitled *The American Sex Revolution* (Boston, 1956).

4. The word *pagan* owes its origin to the Latin *pagus* (village, county), pointing to the urban character of practices which early Christians observed while paganism retreated, as it were, to the countryside.

5. Bernath, Klaus, *Anima Forma Corporis*, cited previously.

6. References to "Zeitgeist" in the author's book *Entchristlichung und Sexualisierung*.

7. Giese, Hans and Schmidt, Gunter, *Studenten-Sexualität* (Reinbek, 1968). Deals with sexual behavior on the part of male and female students, based on a survey of 3,666 students.

8. *Der Spiegel,* No. 37 (1968).

9. There are many examples of a type of cultural pessimism that tend to satanize our era as being "sexualized." One example is Schlink, M. Basilea and Baginski, Helmut: *Tatsachen sprechen* (Darmstadt-Eberstadt, 1966).

10. For the following passage, see *Der Spiegel,* No. 13 (1971).

11. *Der Spiegel,* No. 11 (1970).

12. See Note 13 with preceding chapter, "Pornography," concerning student response to sexual stimuli.

13. Although Alex Comfort may be guilty of a certain amount of exaggeration, one can agree with his viewpoint that no sexual behavior that does not cause injury may be labeled as unacceptable or sinful.

IV. SEXUALITY AND RELIGION

16. Humanae Vitae *and Its Critics*

1. An English translation of *Humanae Vitae* has been published by the United States Catholic Conference, Washington, D.C.

2. Savramis, *Entchristlichung und Sexualisierung.*

3. These slogans were displayed on posters during the 82nd Catholic Day in the West German city of Essen, September 4–8, 1968.

4. Seeber, David Andreas (ed.), *Katholikentag im Widerspruch* (Freiburg, 1968).

5. Ibid.

6. Ibid.

7. Ibid.

8. Savramis (see Note 2).

9. See chapter on "Theology and Sexuality."

10. In addition to the well-known Encyclical *Casti Connubii* (1931), the Encyclical *Mater et Magistra* (1961), issued by Pope John XXIII, should be noted.

11. It is remarkable that as progressive a Pope as John XXIII could have issued a declaration referring to the "population explosion" in the "Third World," which expressed purely irrational and emotional viewpoints.

12. *Publik* (January 29, 1971).

13. Ibid.

14. *Populorum Progressio,* issued by Pope Paul VI, 1967. A Hong Kong newspaper, quoted in *Der Spiegel,* No. 50 (1970), stated correctly that the Pope should refrain from addressing overpopu-

lated countries as long as he did not revise his negative attitude toward birth control measures.

15. Matthew 5:33–37.
16. Ibid.
17. Second Vatican Council, Article 51.
18. Ibid.
19. Peace Encyclical by Pope John XXIII, *Pacem in Terris*, 1963.

17. Revolt of the Priests

1. Romans 14:23.
2. Jansen, J., *Culturzustände des deutschen Volkes seit dem Ausgang des Mittelalters bis zum Beginn des dreissigjährigen Krieges* (Freiburg, 1894).
3. II Corinthians 3:17.
4. Kavanaugh, James, *A Modern Priest Looks at His Outdated Church* (New York, 1967).
5. Documentation of the Chur meeting, including *Mitteilungen der Solidaritätsgruppe katholischer Priester* (September 19, 1969).
6. Ibid. "At Chur there was, in fact, created a world-wide community of priests, determined to engage in joint thought and joint action."
7. Ibid.
8. Ibid.
9. Long, George, *All I Could Never Be* (London, 1967), as well as Davis, Charles, *A Question of Conscience* (London, 1967).
10. The number of "fallen" priests who broke their vows in order to marry is not known. Estimates in 1967 placed at 10,000 the number of priests who asked to be relieved of their positions in order to marry.
11. *Der Spiegel*, No. 3 (1970).
12. Davis, Charles, op. cit. Davis left the Roman Catholic Church and married a Catholic student, Florence Henderson, in an Anglican ceremony.

18. Beyond the Dualism of Matter and Spirit

1. With regard to the following, see Mensching, Gustav, *Volksreligion und Weltreligion* (1938), as well as other writings by the same author (noted below).
2. Mensching, *Die Religion* (Stuttgart, 1959).

3. Ibid. Also, Mensching, *Das Wunder im Glauben und Aber-glauben der Völker* (Leyden, 1957).

4. Savramis, "Wertsysteme in traditionalen und industriellen Gesell-schaften," in *Internationales Jahrbuch für Religionssoziologie,* Vol. 6 (1967).

5. Mensching, *Vergleichende Religionsgeschichte* (Heidelberg, 1949).

6. ——— *Soziologie der Religion* (Bonn, 1947).

7. Ibid.

8. The reformer should be viewed as representing religious author-ity. See Wach, Joachim, *Religionssoziologie* (Tübingen, 1951).

9. Parsons, Talcott, *Toward a General Theory of Action* (New York, 1962). Parsons suggests that the peer group is, in terms of moral value orientation, the ultimate point of reference.

10. Weber, Max, *Soziologische Grundbegriffe* (Tübingen, 1960).

11. ——— *Wirtschaft und Gesellschaft* (Cologne, 1964).

12. Thus the results of individual actions are no longer—to use Parsons' terminology—merely "collective-integrative" but largely "ego-integrative."

13. Viewed this way, such phenomena as "anarchy" and "rebel-lion," which today are associated with the Student Left, gain totally different meanings.

14. While some may regard a multiplicity of children as a misfor-tune, others consider lack of children as a misfortune; or, misfortune may be equated with poverty and, conversely, consumption and affluence may be viewed as a misfortune.

15. We are dealing here with total abandonment of the worldly, of which—in Christian terms—the Mount Athos community is the purest expression (see chapter on "Christianity and Sexuality").

16. A classic example is "ascetic Protestantism." (See also Notes re: chapter on "The Positive Meaning of Asceticism.")

17. I regard as "Materialism" not only dialectical or historic ma-terialism, but generally excessive value placed on the material; i.e., the material, comprehended by tactile means, as a reality in human existence, while the independence of spiritual existence is simul-taneously being denied.

18. A particularly valuable introduction into basic differences be-tween Western and Eastern Man can be found in the German en-cyclopedia, *Rowohlts Deutsche Enzykopädie,* Nos. 246/247: entry

by William S. Haas, entitled "Östliches und Westliches Denken" (Reinbek, 1967).

19. John 3:16. See also, Romans 8:32 and John 4:9.

20. As stated by Athanasios the Great. See Migne, J. P., *Patrologiae cursus completus* (Paris, 1857).

21. See chapter on "Church and Sexuality."

22. See Note 4.

19. The Positive Meaning of Asceticism

1. See chapter on "Church and Sexuality."

2. For biographical sources on asceticism, see *Die Religion in Geschichte und Gegenwart,* Vol. 1, Columns 639–48 (Tübingen, 1957).

3. Ibid.

4. Matthew 11:19.

5. Extensive material concerning *Philo* in *Die Religion in Geschichte und Gegenwart* (2).

6. Extensive material concerning *Gnosis* (2, 5).

7. Savramis, *Zur Soziologie des byzantinischen Mönchtums* (Leyden-Cologne, 1962).

8. Schubart, Walter, *Religion und Eros* (Munich, 1941).

9. See chapter on "The Reformation Did Not Take Place."

10. Ibid.

11. Luther, *Der Grosse Katechismus* (various editions).

12. Ibid.

13. Wingren, Gustav, *Luthers Lehre vom Beruf;* cited previously, "A vocation is the *worldly or spiritual* task of the Christian." My emphasis.

14. See Notes re: chapter on "Marriage."

15. The key work in this field is Max Weber's *Die protestantische Ethik und der Geist des Kapitalismus.* A detailed bibliography (pp. 385–400) may be found in Eisenstadt, S. N., *The Protestant Ethic and Modernization: A Comparative View* (New York, 1968).

16. Weber, Max, *Gesammelte Aufsätze zur Religionssoziologie* (Tübingen, 1920).

17. Troeltsch, Ernst, *Die Soziallehren der christlichen Kirchen und Gruppen* (Tübingen, 1912).

18. Bienert, Walther, *Die Arbeit nach der Bibel* (Stuttgart, 1954).

19. See Note 16.

20. See Note 15.
21. Müller-Armack, Alfred, *Religion und Wirtschaft* (Stuttgart, 1959).
22. See Note 16.
23. Weber, *Wirtschaft und Gesellschaft* (Tübingen, 1956).
24. ——— *Gesammelte Aufsätze zur Religionssoziologie* (16).

20. Sex and Religion: Can the Rift Be Closed?

1. Weber, Max, *Gesammelte Aufsätze zur Religionssoziologie*, cited previously.
2. We speak here of values as they reflect the convictions or ideas of an individual, group or society to the extent that they influence decisions that control the behavior of an individual, group or society.
3. Savramis, "Wertsysteme . . ."
4. The most thorough and revealing empirical study of the attitude of priests regarding celibacy is a Dutch survey edited by Osmund Schreuder and published in a German translation under the title, *Der alarmierende Trend: Ergebnisse einer Umfrage beim gesamten holländischen Klerus* (Mainz, 1970).
5. *Der Spiegel,* No. 46 (1967).
6. Ibid.
7. *Publik* (February 17, 1970).
8. *Wahrhaftigkeit: Zur Zukunft der Kirche* (Freiburg-Basle-Vienna, 1969).
9. Davis, Charles, cited previously; also, biographical data re: chapter on "Revolt of the Priests."
10. My emphasis.
11. I Corinthians 14.
12. I Corinthians 12:28.
13. New York, 1971.
14. See Notes re: chapter on "Christianity and Sexuality."
15. *Der Spiegel,* No. 5 (1971).
16. Ibid.
17. Koch, Friedrich, *Negative und Positive Sexualerziehung: Eine Analyse katholischer, evangelischer und überkonfessioneller Aufklärungsschriften* (Heidelberg, 1971).
18. Ibid.
19. As quoted by Koch.

20. Ibid.

21. Ibid.

22. *Der Spiegel*, No. 8 (1970); *Publik* (February 13, 1970).

23. *Die Zeit* (January 8, 1971), "Aufruf zum Kirchenkampf," and *Publik* (January 8, 1971), "Kirchen-Staat-Moral."

V. SEXUALITY BETWEEN RELIGION AND SOCIETY

21. Results of Christian Antagonism to Sex

1. Van Ussel, J., *Sexualunterdrückung: Geschichte der Sexualfeind-schaft* (Reinbek, 1968).

2. Cited by Reich, Wilhelm, *The Mass Psychology of Fascism* (New York, 1946).

3. *Der Spiegel*, No. 29 (1970).

4. Ibid.

5. Ibid.

6. Thomas, Klaus, *Handbuch der Selbstmordverhütung* (Stuttgart).

7. —— *Sexualerziehung* (Stuttgart, 1964).

8. Neill, A. S., *Summerhill* (New York, 1960).

9. Ibid.

10. See Note 7.

11. Thomas devotes the eighth chapter of his book to the treatment of suicide-prone individuals, with special reference to "ecclesiogene neurosis."

12. Ibid.

13. *Der Spiegel*, No. 3 (1970).

14. *Publik* (May 1, 1970).

15. *Der Spiegel*, No. 3 (1970).

16. Issued at St. Peter's in Rome, March 31, 1970.

17. Herbort, Heinz Josef, "Der päpstliche Mischehenerlass stösst auf Kritik," in *Die Zeit* (May 8, 1970).

22. Between Religion and Government

1. As cited by Holzer, Horst, "Sexualität und Herrschaft," in *Soziale Welt*, Vol. 20 (1969).

2. Ibid.

3. Tommaso Campanella (1568–1639).

4. *Sonnenstaat* (*Sun State*). Related literature in Neusüss, Arnhelm

(ed.): *Utopie: Begriff und Phänomene des Utopischen* (Neuwied and Berlin, 1968).

5. Savramis, *Theologie und Gesellschaft* (Munich, 1971).

6. Heinisch, Klaus J.

7. As quoted by Heinisch.

8. Ibid.

9. Ibid. My emphasis.

10. Pseudonym of Eric Blair (1903–50).

11. Haw, J. M., *Eine gute Beichte* (Leutesdorf, 1935).

12. Ibid.

13. *Die Zeit* (April 16, 1971).

14. *Der Spiegel*, No. 50 (1970).

23. *Sex and Freedom*

1. Savramis, *Religionssoziologie: Eine Einführung* (Munich, 1968); by the same author, *Entchristlichung und Sexualisierung*, previously cited.

2. Literature concerning the concept of freedom is, of course, extensive. One English-language work—not necessarily representative of available sources—is Berdayev, N., *Slavery and Freedom* (London, 1944).

3. Van Ussel, J., *Sexualunterdrückung*, cited previously.

4. Philipp, Wolfgang, *Weibwertung oder Muterrecht?* (Königsberg-Berlin, 1942).

5. Friedrich, Theodor, *Formenwandel von Frauenwesen und Frauenbildung* (Berlin, 1934).

6. Ibid.

7. Von Unruh, Fritz, *Nationalsozialismus* (Frankfurt, 1931).

8. Hitler, Adolf, *Mein Kampf* (Munich, 1941).

9. Cited in Hofer, Walther, *Der Nationalsozialismus* (Frankfurt, 1957).

10. See chapter on "The Satanization of Women."

11. Savramis, *Entchristlichung*, etc.

12. 61st printing (Berlin, 1964).

13. Ibid. Author's emphasis.

14. Ibid.

15. The Vatican newspaper, *Osservatore Romano*, stated on March 2, 1970, that "sexual revolution" and social democracy appear to go hand-in-hand; citing Scandinavian and British examples, it con-

cluded: "The forward movement of Eroticism in Germany stands in direct relation to the forward movement of Social Democracy." See also, *Der Spiegel*, No. 33 (1970).

16. Radhakrishnan, S., *Religion und Gesellschaft* (Darmstadt and Geneva, undated).

24. Man Comes of Age

1. Bebel states in his book on woman and socialism, cited previously, that "a society that rests on total, democratic equality cannot permit oppression of any kind."

2. To the point is the Polish philosopher Leszek Kolakowski, who calls Stalinism "a caricature of Nazism with Marxist phraseology." Quoted in *Der Spiegel*, No. 22 (1969).

3. *Der Spiegel*, No. 36 (1970).

4. With regard to the following, see *Der Spiegel*, ibid., "Sowjet-Union: Hinter dem Vorhang."

5. *Der Spiegel*, ibid.: "Marriage counselor Frau Baskina seemed to prefer offering practical household hints to suggestions providing sex education. Young girls were advised to practice less sewing and darning but bake cakes and prepare cold cuts. Rather than getting involved with old-fashioned skills, they were advised to clean house quickly, use vacuum cleaners and other modern conveniences and learn to prepare a meal 'with a minimum of supplies and by using semi-finished foods.'"

6. Bovet, Th., *Ehekunde* (revised edition, Tübingen, 1963).

7. Weber, Max, *Politik als Beruf* (Berlin, 1964).

8. Tillich, Paul, *Wesen und Wandel des Glaubens* (Berlin, 1961).

25. Religion and Sexuality

1. The work of most lasting value in this field remains Rudolf Otto's *Das Heilige* (*The Sacred*), published originally in 1917. It is a precious and useful aid for an understanding of the sacred, religion and religiosity. Gustav Mensching, in his own work *Die Religion* (Stuttgart, 1959), used this source when he spoke of religion as "the significant encounter with the Sacred and responsive action of man chosen by the Sacred." Some sociologists may view this definition as imprecise, particularly as the word "Sacred" does not specify "what is totally different." This may refer to the sacred as

impersonal as well as personal, male or female. But just because of this, I regard the definition as better than others that tend to exclude sacred reality as a subjective experience, or that in a one-sided manner see the sacred as something quite specific. I believe that one can supplement the definition provided by Mensching with appropriate definitions offered by sociology, the religio-sociological, theology and philosophy. This gives us a variety of definitions which, on the one hand, supplement each other excellently, while, on the other hand, may be useful for different purposes. From the field of sociology I should like to select Talcott Parsons, who delineates religion in its relation to philosophy, ideology and science because he sees religion as a belief system that has the character of non-empirical values (*The Social System*, Glencoe, 1959). Among sociologists of religion, I should like to mention J. M. Yinger, whose useful definition speaks of religion as a system based on faith-images and hopes used by human groups in their encounters with the ultimate problems of life (*Religion, Society and the Individual*, New York, 1960). Additional definitions have been provided, for example, by Tillich.

2. See "Foreword" to this volume.

3. See chapter on "Beyond the Dualism of Matter and Spirit."

4. Cited in *Publik* (September 11, 1970).

5. Krishnamurti, Jiddu, *Education and the Significance of Life* (London, 1968).

INDEX